Shania Twain

On My Way

Shania Twain

ON MY WAY

Dallas Williams

ECW PRESS

We acknowledge the support of the Canada Council
for the Arts for our publishing program.
This book has been published with the assistance
of grants from the Ontario Arts Council.

CANADIAN CATALOGUING IN PUBLICATION DATA

Williams, Dallas, 1967–
Shania Twain : on my way

Includes bibliographical references.
ISBN 1-55022-297-X

1. Twain, Shania. 2. Country musicians –
Canada – Biography. 1. Title.

ML420.T969W72 1997   782.421642'092   C97-931468-2

Front-cover photo: Susan Sterner/AP-Wide World Photos.
Back-cover photo: Steve Granitz/Retna.

Design and imaging by ECW Type & Art, Oakville, Ontario.
Printed by Kromar Printing, Winnipeg, Manitoba.

Distributed in Canada by General Distribution Services,
30 Lesmill Road, Don Mills, Ontario M3B 2T6.

Distributed in the United States by Login Publishers Consortium,
1436 West Randolph Street, Chicago, Illinois, U.S.A. 60607.

Published by ECW PRESS,
2120 Queen Street East, Suite 200,
Toronto, Ontario M4E 1E2.

http://www.ecw.ca/press

PRINTED AND BOUND IN CANADA

ACKNOWLEDGMENTS

I could not have completed this project without the assistance, guidance, support, and love of many people, especially "Loretta" Lynn Crosbie and Tony "Bluegrass" Burgess. The staff of ECW Toronto and Montreal were, as always, invaluable. Special thanks are due to Bill Borgwardt, Paul Davies, Dallas Harrison, Colin Hill, Angelie Kim, Robert Lecker, Holly Potter, and my editor, Mary Williams.

A thousand prayers of thanks to Robert Pollard and all the "golden boys" for keeping me sane.

This book is for my father because he put up with all the racket. And still does.

Contents

1

A STRANGER
IN THE NEW
COUNTRY

Shania (Shuh-NYE-uh):
Ojibwa for "I'm on my way"

Stunning, sexy, and elegant in an evening gown that hugs her petite frame, Shania waits. Tonight she wears her mane of chestnut hair swept high above her beaming face; in the back, it cascades luxuriously below the gentle arc of her bare shoulders. Beside her, French Canadian megastar Céline Dion titters like an ecstatic schoolgirl in a sparkling leopard-print ensemble. The chanteuse's eyes are riveted to a television monitor. The pair stand arm in arm like the best of friends, anxiously anticipating their moment.

Shania has been preparing herself for this since the late 1980s when she first decided to change her name and proclaim to the world "I'm on my way." And now she has arrived. At this very moment, Shania Twain is watching Anne Murray, the Snowbird herself, the most famous Canadian vocalist of all time, pass the torch. It's the evening of 9 March 1997. Canada's annual Juno Awards broadcast is under way. Backstage at the Copps Coliseum in Hamilton, Ontario, Shania and Céline feel their ears burn. The two young women are listening, shyly, to a living legend celebrate *their* achievements.

At home in Lake Placid, New York, Shania harbors Grammy Awards, American Music Awards, and an array of Junos: she's no longer a stranger to success and adulation. But tonight is special. Tonight Shania is one of three proud women — the others are Dion and (an absent) Alanis Morrisette — who will be receiving the inaugural Juno for international achievement. Tonight Shania's native land is rewarding her with a resounding "thank-you."

The audience erupts as Shania and Céline take the stage. The entire auditorium rises to greet the conquering heroines. They are resplendent; bright lights caress and envelop them. A deafening ovation marks this moment, the highlight of the evening. The joy of these two women is palpable and infectious as they clasp one another's hands and triumphantly raise them high in the air. Despite everything, Shania has made it.

As she returns backstage, Shania suddenly appears drained. Emotionally exhausted. An audacious reporter pesters her with questions about her heritage. She is curt but not unkind in her weary response: "I'm Native. Take it or leave it" (Renzetti). The moment is an awkward one, but Shania's answer puts the whole evening into perspective. At the sweet crest of her success, she resolutely honors her family. This woman, whose life story sounds like something penned by Hank Williams himself, an honest-to-goodness hurting song, credits her origins.

★ ★ ★

Motor City. Detroit, Michigan. This blue-collar town, this Great Lakes port, has been called a lot of things over the years. Famed for its contributions to the auto industry, notorious for its history of violent crime, legendary for landmarks like the Paradise Club, and celebrated for the funky groove or angelic, sultry harmonies of its jazz, blues, gospel, and soul, Detroit is a working-class music capital. Many things to many people, it's even been dubbed Rock City in heavy-metal lyrics. Home of Motown, the MC5, and Patti Smith, the Lions, Tigers, Pistons, and Red Wings, Detroit's never been confused with Nashville: a northern town, through and through, it just can't be considered a country-music hotbed. In short, Detroit's an unlikely place for one of country music's most astonishing and heartwarming success stories to begin. But, then again . . .

A border city, Detroit is one of those places that act as conduits for Canadians seeking a way into American culture. Windsor, Ontario, a factory and university town, is just across the Detroit River: the two-way traffic between these points flows easily; it's a well-established routine. On any given Friday night, clubs and concert halls in Detroit are filled with Canadian music fans. Motor City sports arenas are patronized by hordes of Canadian season ticket holders who would rather never see another game than swear allegiance to a Toronto or Montreal team.

Living, as they do, in the nerve center of the Canadian auto industry, Windsorites can't help but see Motowners as a kind of extended family. The link is undeniable: if you're from Windsor, you have access to a mainline that will carry you, via Detroit, straight to the heart of America. The influence radiating from that heart is huge. Windsor natives have to struggle to maintain a distinct, unique identity in the face of it. Some of the kids born north of the border grow up thinking that if they're going to make their mark on the world, if they're going to be rich or famous or influential, they're going to have to break into Detroit first. And that's only natural. The larger town is magnetic and layered with legend. Canadians, especially border-town dwellers, often display ambivalence towards their monolithic neighbor to the south. In Windsor, this attitude is almost palpable. Windsorites are attracted to the U.S., yet frightened by it as well. It's so familiar, but it's also intractably foreign. Windsor, it seems, longs to make contributions to American culture as much as it needs to assert its Canadian identity. In the mid-sixties, the town did both — without even realizing it.

The Beatles had landed. Vietnam was still a minor annoyance confined to a remote part of the world that many North Americans would have had trouble locating on a globe. The Summer of Love was a couple of years off. Country music was still called Country and Western, and few people north of the Mason-Dixon Line thought of the country-music world as anything more than a haven for cowboy hats, pedal steel guitars, tumbleweeds, and broken hearts. In Windsor, however, the seeds of change had been sown, and the history of country music was to reap the benefits.

Sharon Edwards was pregnant — very pregnant with her second child. It had been a long, hot summer. Sharon, her husband, Clarence Edwards, and their daughter, Jill, were anxious to find out whether the new addition to their small family would be a boy or a girl. On 28 August 1965, the wait was over. Eileen Regina Edwards was born.

Why is the birth of this baby girl significant? After all, the name Eileen Edwards rings no bells for most people.

The answer is, because of who she becomes. Because she'll be fortunate enough to have a chance at rebirth, to remake herself twice, three times. Because she'll become Eileen Twain. And because Eileen Twain will discover and become the woman the world now knows as country-music superstar Shania Twain.

Eileen wouldn't adopt that name for another two and a half decades, and she would leave Windsor by the time she was two, but she did come into a world imbued with the powerful influence of American culture — it was constant and inescapable. From birth, it called to her, even as the roots of her Canadian identity took hold in her native soil. The road to Nashville and country-music stardom began just beyond the customs and immigration post that separates Ontario and Michigan. For Eileen Edwards, Detroit was just the first of many way stations on that road. But the journey south, however alluring, would prove an arduous one for Eileen, an odyssey filled with so many pitfalls, roadblocks, and tragedies that no one would have been surprised if she had abandoned it before it had even begun.

Shortly after Eileen turned two, just after her baby sister, Carrie-Ann, was born, Sharon and Clarence's shaky marriage faltered and crumbled. In due course, Sharon packed up her things, prepared her daughters, and left Windsor forever. For the first time in what was to become a long period of travel and displacement, Eileen was on the move. She would never get to know the town in which she was born. Clarence Edwards disappeared from her life, following his own path. Eileen would never really get to know him, either; it was not until almost thirty years later that she would publicly acknowledge his existence. Her life began anew when she quit Windsor. Sharon fell in love again, and took her brood to live in northern Ontario. And there, in the small town of Timmins, Eileen Edwards became little Eileen Twain.

★ ★ ★

In so many ways, Shania's bio reads like a fairy tale. She has often described her life as "a dream come true." In fact, she's Cinderella and Snow White rolled into one — hers is the rags-to-riches story to beat them all. She's a working-class hero with the voice of an angel. Her pure and extraordinary talent is combined with the desire, savvy, and work ethic of the seasoned professional. A sultry, smoldering beauty whom the cameras adore, she exudes a homespun charm — one part grace and one part simple honesty — that has elicited the respect and adoration of her audiences. She was blessed. It was fated. Shania Twain was destined for this.

But what is this? What's Shania got that no one else has? What is it about her? What's her story? On a superficial level, it seems stitched together from every cliché imaginable. Unparalleled success. Happiness. Love. The world in the palm of her hand. She's lived up to the promise of her Ojibwa name: every record she's sold — over twelve million worldwide — bolsters her assertion that "I'm on my way." In fact, she's arrived. And as the saga of how she got here unfolds, the clichés of how she got here expand and collapse, and an image of a living, breathing woman is revealed.

The tale begins when Shania was just Eileen, a precocious little girl living in northern Ontario, and later a young adult burdened with a staggering load of familial responsibilities in the cottage resort town of Huntsville. It was a time before all the videos and awards, the profiles in *Time* and *Newsweek*. Before she graced the cover of *Chatelaine*. Before her Oprah and Letterman and Leno

TODD KOROL/AP–WIDE WORLD PHOTOS

appearances. Before screaming throngs jostled for a glimpse of her at fan-fair meet-and-greets. Before she was installed on a Macy's Thanksgiving Day parade float, or opened Vancouver's BC Place stadium, or met and performed for the Clintons. Before all of this, there was a time when Shania was as alien to America as America was to her.

Today, in so many respects, Shania Twain is living the American dream. She's built the ranch house and studio on a three-thousand-acre estate in New York's Adirondack Mountains, she has a 2.5-carat diamond ring, a couple of horses, a few dogs, and a storybook marriage. Throw in a white picket fence and two kids and you have an image of Norman Rockwell perfection. But there's more. For thousands of young men, Shania has become an object of desire. For women all over North America and Europe, she has become an idol. She has sold more records more quickly than any other artist in country-music history. She is, in fact, the embodiment of New Country. As DJ Cliff Dumas, morning man at CISS FM, Canada's premier country radio station, says, "Anne Murray cracked the door to success in America. Michelle Wright wedged it a little more. Shania blew it open" (Schneller). Greg Haraldson, Calgary station CKRY director of programming, agrees: "Part of the success of country music today is sex appeal. And Shania's incredibly sexy" (Jennings).

She has changed American country music forever because of this indisputable, time-tested fact: sex sells. For decades, character, traditional values, confession, and tragedy dominated this music-industry niche, spawning a relatively small but fiercely loyal fan base that identified wholeheartedly with its musical heroes and heroines. Until the late eighties, country-music superstars were still good ol' boys and gals whom record buyers recognized as their own kind of people. But then the era of the heartthrobs and bombshells dawned. Billy Ray Cyrus — seemingly destined to be a one-hit wonder until his most recent release, *Trail of Tears*, met with critical acclaim — took America by storm with his poster-boy looks, gyrating hips, and a catchy pop marketing strategy. Country crossed over and took off. All of a sudden, image and a pretty face were as important as the songs themselves. As soon as country became sexy, its appeal grew exponentially; radio stations and video channels jumped on the bandwagon, feeding the phenomenon with serious advertising dollars.

It's happened to scores of pop and rock artists over the years, but Shania Twain may be the first country performer to achieve superstar status based largely on her image. Some critics have tried to downplay her success by calling her "a female bimbo Billy Ray" (Cohen), but Lucinda Chodan, a writer for *Country* magazine, puts their nastiness into perspective and hits the nail on the head when she notes that, "If Billy Ray Cyrus introduced sex appeal to country music, Shania has moved things along to a first-name basis" ("Twain's World"). Undeniably, people were struck by the total Shania package before they truly appreciated her songs. In the extensive thank-you list included in the liner notes of her breakthrough second album, *The Woman in Me*, Shania acknowledges that even before she achieved success she'd understood how important radio, television, and video would be to her career. Her promotional plans and strategies were set firmly at the starting line, and Shania has consistently demonstrated a fundamental understanding of one of the most famous theories put forward by another internationally influential Canadian, cultural theorist and pundit

Marshall McLuhan: for her, the "medium" really is a big part of the "message."

Before any of the songs on her album ever hit the airwaves, Shania wrote, "I can't thank all the radio stations in North America and around the world enough for your support." She goes on to acknowledge the even more important role of "TNN, CMT, CMT Europe, and all the other video channels out there. My fan letters say it all. You guys and gals are my lifeline to my fans" (liner notes). Of course, Shania is ostensibly giving all the video programmers out there their due for their contribution to the moderate, qualified success of her debut album, *Shania Twain*. But her industry thank-you roster is just as significant for the way it reads in retrospect: the electronic media really were responsible for giving her access to America. They made her second album a stunning success.

When Shania chose not to mount a promotional tour for *The Woman in Me*, she must have known that her controversial decision would mean that she would have to create and maintain a public profile in other ways. And, although the strategy would backfire and begin to haunt her — nagging doubts and rumors about Shania's ability to sing her own songs in a live concert setting persist because skeptics leap at the opportunity of exposing cultural icons as frauds — it has enveloped her in a marketable aura of mystery. *Come on Over*, the as yet to be released follow-up to *The Woman in Me*, is even more eagerly anticipated because Shania has promised to tour in the near future. To date, fans and critics alike have only been able to glimpse the star in action in a limited capacity — at fan fairs, on awards shows, or on video.

The selling of *The Woman in Me* has had everything to do with making the best possible use of Shania's remarkable beauty. From the album art, to the clothes she wears in public, to the ways she's been directed in the album's eight videos, Shania has been presented as simultaneously sultry and earthy; the way she looks into a camera is at once provocative and innocent, and it's a deadly combination. This, allied with the tough wit and sass of her lyrics and the groundbreaking, pop-rock influenced production values of her catchy music, has made her irresistible. The likes of actor-director Sean Penn, photographer-filmmaker John Derek, and even Shania's own producer-husband, Robert John "Mutt" Lange, have all realized her incredible potential. In helping her manage her image, they've made it almost impossible for America to say no to Shania Twain.

Her physical appearance, then, has opened doors. But it's because of her talent and personality that she's been drawn inside those doors and embraced. The sexy John Derek-directed video for "Whose Bed Have Your Boots Been Under?" her first hit single, didn't just work because Shania looks so good: the song itself is captivating. The clip is saucy, flirtatious, and fun-loving; Shania lights up the small screen. The camera loves her, and she loves it. She dances around a truckstop diner with a crowd of regular-looking guys, and she's captivating, eminently desirable: clearly, Shania knows how to work her looks for film. Still, none of it would play if the tune didn't cut it. And it does.

At first, however, some music television programmers had misgivings about airing the video. The problem, it seems, was that it was too hot. At Country Music Television, where a committee comprised mainly of women is responsible for screening new material, the clip was taken out of heavy rotation. Mercury Nashville's president explains, "I think their official response was that the video was redundant and boring." But, "We felt that they felt it was a little too sexy and that's why they didn't want to play it much. CMT played it only rarely until the record took off and they deserve absolutely no credit for the success" (Leamer). Yet, in the long run, combining the most country-oriented song on *The Woman in Me* with one of its sexiest videos paid off. CMT's cold feet stalled its progress up *Billboard*'s country charts. It remained stuck at number eleven until the sensuous video for the second single, "Any Man of Mine" — codirected by Derek — aired. "Any Man of Mine" reached number four on the charts by the time the 1995 Nashville Fan Fair got under way. By July of that year, Shania had the number-one country song in America.

Because of the unprecedented achievement of Shania's second album, of course, sales of her debut record, *Shania Twain*, have also picked up. The first record, however, though it was quite a personal accomplishment for Shania, just didn't have the production, sales, and marketing focus that has made her second effort so successful. There are no sultry photos on the cover, and the videos just aren't as sexy. In Shania's view, John Derek's art direction for *The Woman in Me* pushed everything to the limit. In some of the pictures on the CD sleeve, Shania almost looks like Derek's famous wife, Bo. And even though she doesn't sport the cornrows, the shots of her from the neck up, as well as others of her swimming while wearing nothing but a cowboy hat and targeting us with a come-hither stare, are reminiscent of some very famous pictures of Bo when she starred in the movie *10*. But this, Shania says, is about as far as she's willing to go.

"There's a difference between sexy and sexual," she has remarked. "I will never do a sex or hot-steaming love scene in a video or that kind of thing." It's not that she's uncomfortable with her body. Shania knows that the way she looks is an asset, and credits her mother and father for convincing her that shyness wasn't really either modest or productive. Today, she always looks like a woman who is at ease with her self-image, though when she was a teenager in Timmins she favored loose, comfortable clothes and tight-fitting bras that, she says, "really binded me in there. I didn't want to bounce. God forbid I was going to bounce when I walked" ("Twain Says Look"). In the film footage Derek has produced for "Whose Bed Have Your Boots Been Under?" and "Any Man of Mine," there's more than a little bounce in her step. Shania exudes physical confidence. And from there the ball just kept rolling. The fans wanted to see and hear more of this fascinating newcomer, and video after video delivered the goods. Tough Shania, vulnerable Shania, spunky Shania, soulful Shania, rock-and-roll Shania, traditional Shania — it's all there. People came to know her through these clips, these little windows of insight into her character and personality. Ironically, CMT is now one of Shania's biggest supporters. Its director of programming, Tracy Rogers, sings the channel's new tune: "[Shania] has pushed the envelope and broken some rules. . . . She's such a great visual artist; people like looking at her. She's 100 percent babe. But she's talented, too; it's the combination that makes her work" (Cohen).

Once the video train was set in motion, interviews and articles embellished with photos of the ascending star began to sell magazines, and promo material sporting her image — from T-shirts and baseball caps to buttons, calendars, and key-chains — became a hot commodity. Quickly, Shania Twain found herself where she is now: everywhere. The exposure meant that she could begin to talk about her life, and as soon as she started, the world was hooked. Passing through the filter of her natural sense of humor and her down-to-earth worldview, her stories of tragedy, trepidation, and triumph emerged as thoroughly compelling narratives.

In little more than two years, from the time she released her first album on Nashville's Mercury label to the moment it became clear to everyone involved that *The Woman in Me* was going to be a monster hit, Shania Twain had conquered America and become a household name. Not bad for a little girl from Timmins who by all rights should have been crushed by the obstacles life had thrown in her path. This fairy-tale scenario must have been unimaginable for her as a young girl locked in the grip of poverty. Her success, considering her unpromising origins, is even more poignant in light of the fact that she had to achieve so much on her own. Because if being a desperately poor member of a large Native family living light years away from the American cultural mainstream in the rugged Canadian North wasn't difficult enough, the events of 1 November 1987 should have dashed any prospects young Eileen may have had of transcending her circumstances.

It was on that tragic autumn night, the worst of her life, that she received the devastating news from her older sister, Jill: their mother and stepfather had been killed in a head-on collision. Shania and her four siblings were suddenly orphans. The crash changed everything. Shania was thrust, rapidly and unexpectedly, into a position of great responsibility. In one horrible moment her life was transformed. For a second she had been a woman of twenty-two contemplating just how she could parlay her love for music into a viable career; the next instant she was, for all intents and purposes, a parent and primary breadwinner. No one else was willing or able to fulfill those roles, and so Shania became the head of the Twain

RON WOLFSON/LONDON FEATURES

family. There was no more time for dreaming. Her sole focus now was survival.

But what a difference ten years have made. A blend of careful management, good luck, and raw talent has made it possible for Shania to contribute significantly to both Canadian and American cultures. Canadians and Americans alike have showered her with awards and accolades: from Grammys to Junos, she's got all the most important statuettes on her mantle. In Canada, she's proudly hailed as one of the nation's most successful exports. South of the world's longest undefended border, she's been welcomed with open arms, virtually adopted, as a favorite daughter and one of the new icons of American country music. The mutual assimilation has been accomplished with relative ease — it's as if Shania and America were made for one another.

Not that the process was always a completely natural one. "When I first came to America," Shania admits, "I felt like an outsider. That was because I was used to Canada, and I had all these aspects of American culture to get acquainted with. . . . After the first record came out, Mercury records put me on tour with Toby Keith and John Brannen — it was called the Triple Play Tour — and that's when I discovered just how little experience I had of American culture and, especially, of country music culture." She supplies us with some examples: "For instance, people couldn't get over the fact that I didn't starch my jeans and have a crease ironed down the middle. Apparently, everyone else starches their jeans." Then, she continues, "there was the time I went into a diner and asked for tea and they gave me iced tea and I didn't know what it was. That was embarrassing. It was amazing travelling through the South and seeing different places, but it took me awhile to get used to it. We would go into

bars and there would be children in the bars. They have
these little wrist tags on. I could not get over that. . . .
Also, in Ontario people do not wear cowboy boots. Some
do. But not everybody. I was going places where everybody dresses the same and I was a little strange because
I didn't" (Richmond). These odd, simple, funny little
differences took some getting used to. At first, the stress
of being a young foreigner trying to make a name for
herself in an overwhelmingly American art form was
daunting. But Shania, indefatigable as always, persisted.

It's not just that America has been, at times, foreign to
Shania. American country-music fans and insiders have
often found *her* to be puzzling and unique. When you ask
big-name country stars a stock interview question like
"What's your favorite place?" you expect the same answers again and again: "home," or "Nashville," or "the
Grand Ole Opry." Shania, however, will often throw you
a curve. She'll say, for example, "Well, my favorite city in
the world is Rome." Just meeting her, in fact, has shattered
many people's illusions. "People," she says, "are surprised
when they meet me because they expect me to have a
southern accent. For some reason, as different as my music
is — for country — people still expect a country girl.
I'm a chameleon . . ." (Powell). It has been this ability to
change her colors while always finding a way to keep
herself well grounded that's nourished her wide popularity. Shania feels that artistic license allows her to explore
a range of sounds and influences in her music, but she'll
always return to country and the "many things" she loves
about it. "As a performer," she says, "it's what I'm the most
comfortable with. It's also the lifestyle I'm most comfortable with. It's just not an eccentric world. Plus, these days,
because country music is becoming broader, you can
experiment" (Powell).

Shania is in the vanguard in this respect; in fact, the chances she's taken are partially responsible for the broadening and experimentation she talks about. Shania points out, though, that it didn't take a Canadian girl to initiate the change. She believes that American country had already been shown the path she's following by some of its most beloved traditional performers. The spirit of New Country, Shania asserts, has "taken off." But, she goes on to note, "there were other wild times. Johnny Paycheck did that song 'Take This Job and Shove It' in the '70s. It's just that every kind of music is going for a different spin in the '90s. People say, 'Country music's getting a little more daring now.' And I think, well, yeah, but what about rebels like Johnny Cash, Willie Nelson, and Kris Kristofferson?" (Powell).

Eventually, Shania did come to recognize that her difference was part of her appeal. Being Canadian gave her a unique perspective: the music so near and dear to the heart of America was something she could both love and hold at a critical arm's length. Her detachment would lead her to develop a fresh new sound: *The Woman in Me* took country music to places it had never been before because it dared to break with timeworn traditions. An insider, an American, might never have been willing to take the same kinds of risks. As Shania has maintained, "We've reached so many people with that record. We've reached the country music fans and the people who wouldn't normally listen to country music. And we've achieved that by making a record that doesn't sound like every other country record on the charts" (Richmond).

Now Shania Twain is literally at home in America. Though no longer a stranger in a strange land, she's still not following well-beaten country-music paths. Never one to do things the easy way, Shania prefers to do them right, thereby maintaining her own peace of mind. Instead of taking up residence in the South, she remains a resolute northerner, choosing to live in secluded upstate New York. Stylistically, she continues to walk the fine line between country and Top 40 pop: her management and her producer are more familiar with the world of stadium rock than the hallowed venues of Nashville.

Such high-wire acts are hard to pull off in Music City. Remember that Nashville and the American country-music industry constitute a tight-knit and somewhat exclusive community. In 1974, when Australian singer, and star of the film *Grease*, Olivia Newton-John won the Country Music Association Female Vocalist of the Year award over titans like Tammy Wynette, Loretta Lynn, Tanya Tucker, and Dolly Parton, some members left the academy in protest. They resented the idea that an out-sider had gained access to their inner circle. Shania, however, believes that some progress has been made: "I think things have changed a great deal in country music. A lot of industry people in Nashville aren't from Nash-ville. People sometimes underestimate Nashville now and expect it to be resistant to outsiders. . . . My roots are quite deep within country music. That's where I started in the first place, and I think people realize that" (Chodan, "Twain's World").

True, there's an unmistakable country edge to every-thing Shania does. Her attitude towards self-promotion, her conviction that artists must preserve their individu-ality and a certain private space, her devotion to her fans: all this is born of a down-home belief in the value of remaining true to one's roots. With all the sincerity and ingenuousness of a small-town girl, she's been careful not to cultivate a supersize ego to match her superstar status.

The price of stardom, however, can often be one's

personal equilibrium, and Shania has been candid in expressing her disapproval of the way the phenomenon of celebrity has affected some of her peers in the music industry. Reflecting on her own achievement, she concedes, "You have to work very, very hard and live through a life that seems glamorous but really isn't." Some stars, she suggests, are less than honest, both with the public and with themselves. And those who chronicle their lives are often complicit in the deception. Shania remarks: "I was reading an article where it said, 'We caught so-and-so relaxing in the garden and going for a little stroll,' and I thought, 'No, you didn't. This was a booked session, and you spent three hours at this person's home, and they weren't relaxing and they weren't going for a stroll in their garden. They had to have a wardrobe set up, they had to have hair and makeup set up, they were told because of the light where they should be walking and where they should be sitting.' These are the things that the fans aren't supposed to realize, but as the artist speaking, these are the things that can be very, very tiring. There is no time for a leisurely walk through the garden" (Chodan, "Shania Twain Takes Quebec"). For Shania, it has increasingly become important to be realistic about the demands she places on herself, to find the private time she knows that she needs.

Keeping a level head is the key. Even after reaching sales figures that topped the seven-million mark, she still commented that her success felt strange. "Sometimes I think about it," she says, "and it stops me in my tracks. . . . I'm dealing with it as well as I can. If you ask me about it in a year or two's time I'll probably be going crazy. I'll probably be a wreck by then. But at the moment there is still a little bit of a novelty value attached to it all. I don't mind people recognizing me, and I'm anxious not to fall into that big star trap you hear about." Even so, she realizes there are simple things that she can no longer do, and there's real regret in her voice when she talks about, for instance, not being able to go out and buy her own groceries without some form of camouflage. "I have to," she laments, "otherwise I really wouldn't be able to get anything done. I've worked out a few ways to make my-self look completely different without looking like I'm Shania Twain in disguise" (Richmond).

Being high profile in America, garnering the praise, riches, and celebrity due an individual with the power to sell over ten million records, has also meant being subjected to relentless scrutiny. There can be no more secrets. At the peak of her success, Shania has been assailed by scandalmongers bent on discrediting her personal integrity and that of members of her family. Mainstream media organs and the major tabloids jumped into action when her brothers and sister tangled with the law. And when it was revealed that Shania had not been completely forthcoming about her Native heritage, she was raked over the coals by those who insisted she was using her adopted Ojibwa ancestry as a promotional ploy. Shania met her attackers and detractors head-on and never backed down. Her crisis management was classy — and it worked.

All of this, however, belongs to a later chapter in Shania's story. By the time she was called upon to put out such fires, she had transformed herself into a consummate professional with the strength and skill to perform the task. In order to understand that complex and difficult transformation, we have to go back in time — almost thirty years — to an improbable setting: Timmins, Ontario.

2

MUSTARD, MATTAGAMI, AND MOXIE

Rags. A fact of poverty. It's a brutally cold winter morning, and Shania has a full day of school ahead. After that, she'll work an evening shift at McDonald's. In a short while, she'll brace herself for the walk and make her way through snowbound streets in clothes that are clean but not the least bit "cool." Clothes that, though she won't complain, are probably not even warm enough. The first bell will ring at Timmins High and Vocational in an hour. But right now, Shania has work to do.

Her stepfather, Jerry, left for the bush at the crack of dawn. Her mother, Sharon, is still asleep because she's going through it again. Too depressed to get out of bed, she'll be huddled under the blankets until long after Shania hits the books. The three youngest children are rambunctious and hungry. Shania's the one making sure that Mark and Darryl, her little brothers (Sharon and Jerry's offspring), turn off the cartoons and brush their teeth. She's the one drinking water so that little Carrie-Ann, who's growing like a weed again, can have the last glass of milk. When the kids get too loud and threaten to

Shania's old home in Timmins
RACHELE LABRECQUE

disturb Sharon, Shania hushes them by saying that their mom's sick and needs her sleep. They listen. Their big sister inspects them and sends them on their way with a good-bye kiss.

Once Shania's in class, she reverts to being a typical kid. She's finally, though briefly, able to relax into friendships, gossip. She can vent her annoyance at being saddled with so much homework and share her anxiety over impending exams. Somewhere in the back of her head, however, a nagging thought persists: What are we going to eat tonight? Then lunch worries begin to intrude. She often doesn't bring anything to eat, and has come to dread the sly looks and concerned whispers of fellow students and teachers alike.

Later in life, she would admit that she'd often pretend she just wasn't hungry, because she was afraid a teacher would become suspicious and initiate some kind of investigation that might lead a welfare agency to "split up her family" (Lague). Really afraid. The thought was too much to bear: family meant the world to her, and she was unable to imagine living without her brothers and sisters, without her mom and dad. Shania would try to put it out of her head, but that nightmare scenario was tenacious; the fear it generated was hard to shake, and it was regularly triggered by such a benign custom — the midday meal. "We were really poor, although I never considered it that bad. We would go for days with just bread and milk and sugar — heat it up in a pot. I'd judge other kids' wealth by their lunches. If a kid had baked goods, that was like, oh, they must be rich" (Keyes).

Still, the Twains' very real and grinding poverty had an inspirational dimension. It was an early test of Shania's character. "In my house," she says, "it was so wrong to take more than your share. If you decided to take an extra potato, someone didn't get a potato at all. To us, eating like that was only on TV" (Schneller). And, after all was said and done, it brought the family closer together. Individually, they learned the importance of self-sacrifice for the common good. The Twain children understood that, together, as a family unit, they were stronger. This meant that Shania willingly shouldered burdens that many children are spared. Like feeding other kids. She had to accept that at times she would have to be the primary caregiver.

When cooking, cleaning, or ministering to little scrapes and bruises were required, the Twains could count on Shania. Whenever Sharon was incapacitated, in need of her help, she was there. "I ironed Dad's clothes and made porridge in the morning for the kids," she says (Lague). And Shania did it all without complaint because it needed to be done. At an early age she became proficient at a number of dull but necessary domestic duties, and this helped instill in her a sense of real responsibility. When called upon, she became a surrogate parent to her younger siblings, assumed some of the roles that Sharon would have been expected to play, and assisted Jerry with the difficult task of providing for the family. All of this would serve as training for an even more arduous test of her fortitude and maturity, for the time when, tragically, she would be called upon to head this family alone.

Shania, though, is not bitter; instead, she's wise, practical, and caring. She's philosophical about poverty in general, and the way it shaped her life. "I would go over to [friend] Laura [Surch's] house for milk and cookies," she recalls, "and not be able to reciprocate. I didn't bring anyone home until high school, because I didn't want people to know. The one thing I could have done without as a kid was the humiliation of not being able to eat, not bringing a lunch to school. Hunger is much more emotional than physical, you know. You want to keep the other kids, particularly the teacher, from inquiring. You say, 'Oh, I forgot my lunch at home.' Or, 'Oh, I'm just not hungry.' Eventually you run out of excuses. I used to take mustard sandwiches to school, just to have something. It could have been cardboard. No kid should have to go through that" (Keyes).

But Shania, like all the Twain children, did go through it. The truth is, there were times when her family had trouble making ends meet. They were often dirt poor. As a child, Shania would try to keep their circumstances a secret from the outside world. "I did a good job too," she says. "But you know what? I recognized as a kid that I wasn't the worst off. My mother had a lot of pride. We never went to school dirty or in ripped clothes. I always think of 'Coat of Many Colors,' the Dolly Parton song? So when I would see another kid that was dirty, I knew they didn't have the loving parents I had" (Schneller). Comfort and ease may have been elusive, but Shania knows that in the most essential way her life was not impoverished: "My parents were loving. We just didn't have any money" (Lague).

★ ★ ★

Her first two winters were spent in relatively temperate Windsor, but by the age of three Shania had been transplanted into a world of toboggans, snowshoes, and tire chains — Canada's frozen North. Timmins, in the winter, can be a frigid, inhospitable place. Shania, with Sharon, Jill, and Carrie-Ann, left Windsor to find a better life with the only father she has ever known: Gerald Twain. A full-blooded Ojibwa who fought all his life to make it as a forester and mining prospector, Jerry was also a devoted husband and an old-fashioned family man who would sacrifice anything for his children. Sharon, a passionate Irish Canadian, was the love of his life.

When she took her girls out of Windsor, Sharon had a great deal to worry about. Would she be able to take care of her three small children? Would they suffer from not having the influence of a father? All her fears were put to rest by Jerry Twain. She adored him and would have followed him to the ends of the earth. Finding Jerry, Sharon felt, erased the mistake of her first marriage. Shania was six when Sharon and Jerry married. Shortly after the wedding, Jerry legally adopted the three girls his wife had had with another man, and resolved to raise them as his own. By marrying Sharon, he made her and all her children members of his band. As Jerry Twain's child, Shania was officially granted First Nations status.

She was, and is, a member of the Temagami Anishnawbe Bear Island First Nation. It didn't matter in the least to Shania that Jerry Twain was not her first father — he was her real father.

In fact, for many years, the issue was never even considered. Phrases like "biological father" just weren't used in the Twain household. Shania and her sisters didn't feel adopted because they were, along with their brothers, Mark and Darryl, all Jerry's kids. No one in the family enjoyed special status. "I grew up in a Native family and always considered myself Native," Shania explains. "We didn't think in terms of a step-father, half-brothers. We were all just family" (Hager). Shania was the apple of Jerry's eye. She hated it when Jerry left for work, and when he was home she rarely left his side. Jerry would shower her with attention; he taught her how to trap rabbits so that they could spend more time together. From Jerry, Shania derived pride, self-reliance, and a love of the land. "I want to stay close to what I grew up with," she remarks, in homage to her adoptive father. "I like being secluded. I like solitude. I never want to let go of it. It's a craving for me. I have to be in the bush and it has to be the northern bush" (Dunphy). The bush reminds her of where she comes from, of Jerry and the rest of her family, always inside her, always informing who she is.

In so many ways, she's just like Jerry; more than anything else, Shania is a Twain. That Jerry was an inspiration and a role model is evident in the tough choices Shania has made throughout her life. From her determination to defend her heritage and family at all costs (a determination that becomes such an important element later in her history), to the most basic decisions she's made about how to live from day to day, she follows in Jerry's footsteps. A woman who, despite her unprecedented success, has her feet firmly planted on the ground, Shania has resisted the bright-lights-big-city temptations of Los Angeles and Nashville. She remains, resolutely, the kind of northerner that her father raised her to be. And though she duly credits both Sharon's and Jerry's love of music as influential, Gerald Twain was, in effect, her first music teacher.

Jerry was the kind of amateur guitarist that you'll find haunting the aisles of music stores and record shops in every North American city. He could play well enough to fake his way through a few hits, but he wasn't going to quit his day job and head into the studio. The picking and strumming equivalent of the five- or six-handicap weekend golfer who entertains secret fantasies of taking the Masters title away from Tiger Woods, Jerry was an avid country fan who could feel his way around a fretboard.

He learned his favorite songs by ear, and considered guitar playing a relaxing hobby as well as a communal act, one that, like storytelling, was a perfect way of entertaining friends and family. Shania's natural curiosity inevitably led her to explore music, and Jerry gave her the gift that would launch that exploration: the gift of what knowledge he had. Jerry taught Shania how to hold the guitar, and strum it, and keep it in tune. He showed her where to position her soft little fingers to play her first chords.

The love and respect Shania continues to nurture for her parents are palpable and touching. It's a fact entirely independent of the Shania Twain publicity machine. In interview after interview, she has spoken of her gratitude for their loyalty and unflagging encouragement of her musical aspirations. Sharon and Jerry were the first to recognize her talents; they were her first and biggest fans. Shania equates their love with her love for music. In her earliest memories, she says, the two are blended together:

"I distinctly remember singing when I was three years old. I would go off by myself and sing a song like 'Twinkle, Twinkle,' changing the rhythm and humming different tones" (Hager). Around the same time, her mother became acutely aware of her daughter's talents and proclivities. Sharon would pop tiny Shania onto the counter at a nearby coffeeshop and coax her to sing for the customers. And when Sharon noticed that Jill's classical guitar always seemed to be in Shania's arms, she and Jerry resolved to do everything they could to help her develop her budding talent.

They were proud to expose their little prodigy to the country-music-loving public. At the tender age of eight, Shania began singing in bars. By the time she was ten, she was quite accustomed to playing for a club full of strangers. Jerry and Sharon would wake her late at night, take her from the room she shared with Jill and Carrie-Ann, and drive her to the Mattagami Hotel, in Timmins, where she would sing a selection of country tunes. "I used to be dragged out of bed at 1:00 in the morning and they'd bring me to the local club to play with the band," she recollects. "They weren't drinkers, they just wanted to hear the music. . . . You see, I wasn't even allowed in until they stopped serving alcohol. I'd get up and sing a few songs . . . and before I knew it, I was actually doing clubs professionally" (Keyes).

The pint-sized performer would make her way through the bar, guided by her father or mother. After being boosted onto the stage, she'd set up and take the spotlight, dwarfed by her six-string guitar. The image she presented must have been arresting and a little strange, but for Shania it all became normal very quickly. This was real — and it was hard work. Her style wasn't "cute"; she continues to insist that she was never a novelty act. "I always did adult music," Shania says proudly. "It was an adult world" (Powell).

So as a child *and* as a performer, Shania grew up fast. She was "paying her dues, the way few country singers of the nineties pay them any longer, and she was only eight years old" (Leamer). Today, though, she's not sure that she would have made the same choices if left to her own devices. Looking back, her childhood, a patchwork of extremes, must sometimes seem like a distant dream — something that happened to someone else. All that attention coupled with exasperating hardship would surely have been confusing to a young child. After all, she knew how other children lived and what they desired. Her country-music stardom, Shania acknowledges, was really Sharon and Jerry's goal. "I dreamed," she confesses a little wistfully, "of being a kid" (Lague). It wasn't to be: Shania had to relinquish her childhood not only to meet the domestic demands that the Twain financial predicament had placed on her, but also to embark on an adult career. Her parents were committed to that agenda on her behalf; as Shania herself says, "they made me do it and I just had to" (Cohen).

In time, Shania became very practical about her talents, accepting what her parents told her about the necessity of performing live if she was to develop her natural gift. Experience, they reasoned, would be the best teacher. Backstage before one of those early gigs, Shania remembers them telling her, "You're in an adult world; you can't be a crybaby." They wouldn't allow her to be timid, and petulance was not an option. The other musicians, they pointed out, were not "crying the blues, or shaking in their boots" (Cohen). Shania, of course, knew that they weren't. She was watching carefully. Throughout her early career, she met and/or played with many talented, experienced performers, eventually working bills with such acts as Freddy Fender and the rock band Trooper. "I remember Gary Buck and Dallas Harms," she says. "I used to be on shows as the opener for Anita Perras when I was just a kid and she was a teenager. I opened for people like Carrol Baker. Ronnie Prophet [too]" (Brown). None of these pros had time for the jitters.

So Sharon and Jerry made Shania see that other performers were on stage to enjoy themselves do what they did best. "They're out there," they said, "being professionals." Shania accepted her parents' logic. "I had to live up to that," she says. "Mind over matter, bite the bullet and do it" (Cohen).

She pulled it off. Again, the little girl stood up to adversity and exceeded all expectations. Whether cooking for her siblings, or cleaning house, or performing a country classic for a tavern full of small-town revelers looking to escape the daily pressure cooker for a couple of hours, she responded like an adult. Once the microphone was lowered to accommodate her tiny frame and her guitar was in tune, her reticence disappeared. Her music would fill the room, and she would take charge like a pro. The incredulous house band, the intrigued crowd, her proud, anxious parents, never ceased to be amazed by her poise. Yet it's hard to imagine exactly what those performances could have been like. Just after the release of *The Woman in Me*, an interviewer asked the newly minted star if she'd had to stand on a chair to enable the audience to see her. Shania shed a little more light on those gigs by commenting that what the Timmins tavern-goers saw was mainly her acoustic: "The guitar was bigger than me," she joked. "I wish they would have made those half-width size guitars when I was eight . . . nine . . . ten . . . eleven and twelve. I was so small that they couldn't lie flat on me.

They were sticking out because I couldn't get my arm around them" (Brown).

At the time, her set list included such country standards as Dolly Parton's "Goodbye to Daddy" and "Coat of Many Colors," and Charlie Pride's "Kaw-Liga." Even to a veteran road act, the Mattagami audiences would have seemed tough. Hard-living working-class northerners looking to blow off a little steam couldn't have been inclined to fawn over a preteen cowgirl, or even cut her any slack. But despite the fact that she was, understandably, a little shy, a little reluctant, young Shania managed to come off like a natural. These were her people, and she responded like a born performer. And she was already every bit as tough as any Mattagami Friday-night regular. "It's awkward to be in a bar when everyone's drunk and smoking," she has said, commenting on those early gigs, "but I had to do it anyway" (Brown). Throughout what must have seemed a trial by fire, she excelled, gaining confidence, learning to persevere, and developing her energetic, enthralling stage presence.

As a youngster, Shania couldn't get enough of the music that had so rapidly become her passion: her whole life revolved around country. And this passion wasn't fed by MTV or the Nashville Network; she acquired and extended her musical tastes the old-fashioned way — by listening to the greats. Because Shania grew up just before the advent of the rock video changed the music industry forever, radio was an irreplaceable aspect of her day-to-day routine. Tuning in at a time when country music was far from dominating the airwaves, she didn't limit herself. Top-40 hits were also an inspiration. "I've always listened to Elton John, Stevie Wonder, and the Mamas and Papas," she declares (Powell). Despite Canada's content regulations for radio — which guarantee Canadian musicians a percentage of airtime in an effort to maintain and promote a national culture in the face of stiff and relentless international competition — the wide variety of music to which Shania found herself exposed gave her a sense of a creative world unconstrained by national borders. Country music, like all other genres, has transcended and erased the lines that divide the world into political units. At home in Timmins, Shania could play an album or turn on the radio and access the heart of Nashville. The distance between the two cities dissolved into thin air.

Singers and songwriters, for Shania, weren't American or Canadian. They were just musicians. As a result, she felt no special kinship with other Canadian artists — people like Neil Young and Joni Mitchell were simply famous artists. "Because I started so young," Shania remarks, "I really didn't know who was American and who was Canadian. I didn't necessarily know that Anne Murray or Joni Mitchell were Canadian, I just knew they were on the radio with every other superstar. I didn't spend any time thinking, 'Wow, they're great for Canadians'" (Powell). Achieving this kind of inclusive, international outlook at a very early age has been a boon to Shania: it has equipped her to avoid the pitfalls of feeling like a tiny Canadian fish in a huge, teeming American pond.

In short, Shania was never hindered by an inferiority complex. Unlike so many of her fellow countrymen and women, she never believed that her nationality was an impediment to realizing her dreams. She wasn't over-awed at the prospect of being a small-town girl, a foreigner to boot, trying to make it in the big bad city. Shania just played her music, believing she had every right to be a country performer simply because she loved country and felt it in her bones. She didn't even entertain thoughts about how improbable it all was. She just believed whole-heartedly in that old nugget of wisdom (the essence of the American dream) that you can succeed at anything if you put your mind to it.

Shania would tune in to the radio for hours on end, harmonizing quietly with anything that moved her. She recalls that she "listened to all kinds of music. We had a multi-format station happening in our home town. I heard 'everything' through radio, but at home it was always country. And I only sang country music as a child. I had other influences though. I was really enamoured with the Carpenters, their harmonies . . . were so beau-tiful . . . I learned so much, at a very young age, from groups like that. Karen Carpenter's voice is just like silk, it is so gorgeous!" (Powell).

Shania's is too. It has all of Carpenter's warmth and clarity. The soft but powerful modulations and inflections Shania infuses into the title track of *The Woman in Me*, for example, reveal influences not usually associated with country vocalists. Her sassy edge and plaintive persuasion are often tempered by an MOR sensibility more reminis-cent of pop ballads produced for urban American markets in New York or Los Angeles than a Nashville love song meant to stir emotions in the heartland. Shania's vocal tidal waves would be right at home on a Whitney Houston album; with her understated timing and her technique of swelling one note into another, she takes a page right out of the Carpenter songbook. Still, the finished product has roots in the artist's small-town past.

There's more. *The Woman in Me*, time and time again, pushes the limits of reasonable expectations. In terms of both content and production, it is amazingly fresh — miles ahead of what was standard country fare at the time of its release. Everything from rock to gospel finds its way into the mix, and the effect of the album as a whole forces listeners to redefine the way they understand country music. Sure, there's the twang and drawl that most people expect, but there are also plenty of riffs, rhythms, and vocal nuances that surprise and even shock.

The common thread that links the tracks of this astonishingly diverse album, however, is its creator's singular sensibility. Picking through the vast catalog of everything she knows and loves, Shania has woven a sound that's undeniably her own. And though her style will be emulated for years to come, it's hard to imagine anyone duplicating what she's done on *The Woman in Me*. The record is a product of two decades of apprenticeship with two very different "mentors": this breakthrough album vividly reflects Shania's long association with, and broad understanding of, contemporary music, and her often cruel and trying life experience. A deeply personal work of art, the compilation is both a gateway into her past and the key to understanding who Shania is today. It also provides glimpses of the kind of performer she's destined to become.

Almost every song on *The Woman in Me* is a declaration of independence. The album announces Shania's arrival to the world. It's testimony to her resolve and inner resources. The monster hits "Any Man of Mine" and "Whose Bed Have Your Boots Been Under?" are at once tough, provocative, and vulnerable. They signal the birth of a truly new country, an uncharted musical terrain that's full of urban attitude and working-class grit. The longing of "Home Ain't Where His Heart Is (Anymore)," the joyous power of "You Win My Love," and the hard-earned wisdom of "Leaving Is the Only Way Out" combine to evoke a multifaceted portrait of a self-assured, playful, and emotionally secure young woman who is in control of every aspect of her life. Together, the songs present the woman in Shania with all her complexity, while telling the story, simply and succinctly, of how the little girl from Timmins, Ontario, became Shania Twain.

As the culmination of so many years of development, *The Woman in Me* is a celebration of Shania's roots and her individuality. In May 1994, Shania wrote the first of the two "Fan Letter" columns she has contributed to *Country*, Canada's country-music magazine. Even though it was published while *The Woman in Me* was still being conceived, the remarkable candor of the piece gives us a sense of where Shania's music comes from: "I love remote places and isolation. As a child I would wander off by myself with guitar and matches in hand, to find a quiet spot in the bush or back yard to build a little fire and write songs. If I would hear anyone coming or calling my name, I would be still or quiet as a mouse until they went away. I love people, but I definitely need solitude." Out of that solitude, Shania has created music that's both a private assertion of who she is and a very public gift to the rest of the world.

Behind the mature public persona, however, there was always a young woman wary of scrutiny and reluctant to take center stage. She might have been quite content to go on indulging her love of music tucked away inside those private spaces she created within her heavily popu-lated daily universe if it hadn't been for Jerry and Sharon and the avid interest they displayed in her development as a public performer. Yet Shania will never fault her parents for trying to close up some of those spaces. She firmly believes that their response to her talent was natural and innocent. "I was just always singing with the radio and with the eight-track player in my parents' truck," she confides ("Fan Letter" 1994). "I guess when you hear a six-year-old harmonizing you start to pay attention" (Powell). For a little while, though, music was simply a personal pleasure for Shania — something as intimate and unique as an imaginary friend. Nobody beyond her immediate circle had any idea that Shania was a true musician, and that suited her just fine.

Later, after her duties had expanded to churning out favorites for the late-night crowd at the Mattagami Hotel, she continued to keep part of that private musical persona to herself, inviolate. A note of longing infiltrates her words when she remembers those days: "I was quite happy sitting alone in my room strumming and singing away to Dolly and Merle, or any records or 8-tracks we had at the time," she says (Powell). What was unique, however, was her persistence. The seemingly unlimited sounds she could produce with her guitar and voice were an unending source of fascination for her. Music made her happy. While other kids recoiled from the idea of music lessons and hours of practice, Shania embraced it. Her skills developed by leaps and bounds, and all this hard practical work would eventually meld with her mature imagination and experience to create her trademark sound.

Dedication to craft gave Shania a sense of security and purpose. It made some of the harsh aspects of her life easier to take — in a way, her music became her confessor and best friend, teaching her about who she was, helping her to define her sense of self. Why, then, was she so opposed to sharing with others what she was learning? What was at the root of her aversion to performing? Shania was encouraged to sing from almost the moment she could talk. As a young child, she did believe, quite simply, that music was something to be shared because it was pleasurable. The demise of this innocent, trusting attitude towards performing may actually be traced back to a single disturbing incident that occurred when Shania was in grade 1. She was six years old.

One morning it was her turn to present something for show-and-tell, and she decided to sing. Her selection was "Country Roads." When she finished belting out John Denver's signature tune, her classmates turned on her. They were cruel in that way it seems only children know how to be, making a bewildered and agonized Shania the butt of their derision. "All my classmates," she declares, "thought I was being a 'show off' and it really created serious inhibitions for me." She was deeply hurt.

Worse than their ridicule of her performance was their mocking of her musical taste. They branded her with a nickname, "Twang," and taunted her with it for some time afterwards. Denver's music, and country in general, were just not "in" — and they let Shania know it, loud and clear. Shania came away from the experience believing that "country music wasn't really the thing to sing" (Leamer). All of this was very confusing, partly because it suddenly entered her mind that their reaction was justified. "From that point on, I was afraid to perform. I thought that it was true, in a way, since you do have to do your best and show what you've got when you are performing" — and maybe what she had just wasn't good enough ("Fan Letter" 1994). No matter how much she loved her music, she just couldn't shake the feeling that she should be embarrassed by her performance of it.

That feeling made Shania pine for musical solitude. The memory of the show-and-tell nightmare still bedevils her. She concedes, "I just never got comfortable with 'showing off.' I had to learn how to switch it on and off in my mind. I realized, in time, that people enjoy being entertained and that it was a blessing to be able to make people happy through performing. I still have to use the switch to psyche myself up to get into performance-mode before going on stage, or any other type of performing like interviews or public appearances" ("Fan Letter" 1994).

This type of discomfort was likely behind Shania's decision not to tour *The Woman in Me*, one of the most successful country albums ever. For her, performing before a live audience has clearly become an act of monumental significance. She is convinced that to do it right, to give people their money's worth, you have to give it your all. To be an entertainer is to partake in a kind of sacred trust: the performer is there because of the audience; as soon as the performer allows that situation to be reversed, she has lost her way. In a sense, therefore, Shania's resolving not to tour *The Woman in Me* was an act of self-sacrifice. She felt, at the time, that she didn't have enough to give back to her fans in a live setting. One album of material just wasn't sufficient, and to tour under those circumstances would just be to "show off." The mature superstar was assailed by the same deep-seated misgivings that had undermined the shy little girl.

The negative outburst of Shania's classmates had a further effect: it caused Shania to doubt the validity of her parents' assertion that her music was meant to be shared. A part of her dreaded the idea of having to face the smallest audience of strangers, and she had lost sight of why she even should. But Sharon and Jerry helped their daughter to deal with her anxiety in the most sensible way: when she fell off the performance horse, they helped her right back up. "My parents," she writes in her first "Fan Letter," "really started helping me get over this fear, by putting me up on any and every stage they could find. They had me singing in community centres, homes for the elderly, nightclubs, radio shows, country television shows . . . and family gatherings."

As a musician, Shania grew up fast. Another incident occurred while she was still in grade school that demonstrates both how quickly she was able to revive her self-confidence and how incredibly professional she was for her age. While she was still in grade 5, her school principal invited her to perform at a parent-teacher event. Shania agreed, then laid out some stipulations. "I remember telling him," she says, "that I would need a microphone, a monitor, and a sound system. He didn't know how to respond. Then I told him to call my mother to schedule the performance" (Hager). For one reason or another — Shania can't remember — she didn't end up participating. It is clear, though, that even as a ten-year-old Shania was already taking her career very seriously.

She began composing her own songs before she hit her teens. Initially, of course, they were simple tunes. Driven by a child's wonder at a world that is by turns terrifying and heartbreakingly beautiful, her songwriting developed and began to display real promise as her musical proficiency grew. Even then, people who heard Shania's music were struck by its remarkable maturity. Her family obligations and the pressures of poverty, which dovetailed neatly with the conventional themes of the musical genre she felt closest to, brought Shania into contact with an overwhelmingly adult reality. The sentiments and story lines of her country favorites were as adult as the life she had no choice but to lead. Broken relationships, emotional and physical hardship, betrayal, poverty, never-ending toil — all this formed the thematic substance of the music she was listening to.

But Shania possessed a take-no-prisoners, win-at-all-costs attitude. In country song after country song, men and women gave voice to their trouble and pain, and it all became second nature to Shania. "I never even thought about it," she maintains. "I used to write songs — very adult songs — about love, and people used to say, 'You're ten, how can you write that?' I didn't necessarily relate to the story too well, but I would get into the emotion of singing, so it was convincing, and people would just shake their heads" (Powell).

Twenty years later, the emotional depth of Shania's music still prompts people to shake their heads. And yet there's still something magically childlike about the music she writes. "Writing's like coloring," she says. "Kids like to color, they don't need to have a reason to color — they just like it. Why do they use orange instead of pink, or green instead of blue? I don't know . . . they don't know — they just do. They have no inhibitions. They are totally open to be creative. That's how I feel about songwriting. It's a chance to just create without inhibitions" (Geocites).

"Eileen" Twain, from the 1982–83 Timmins High and Vocational School yearbook

COURTESY DEBBIE M. O'BRIEN SIRARD

But because Shania has triumphed over so much genuine adversity, her songs have a worldly wisdom few other entertainers manage to access. Shania's experience runs deep. That's why there's little sentiment for sentiment's sake in the twelve tracks that make *The Woman in Me* such a stunning songwriting debut. Shania's songwriting is also what makes this album a more compelling one than her first, *Shania Twain*. As she herself has said, "I've always been a songwriter, and I think my delivery is more intimate, more sincere, when I'm not singing someone else's songs" (Chodan, "Twain's World").

As she composed, Shania came to the realization that her voice was as much of an instrument as her guitar. In a workmanlike way, she initiated a course of study and practice that would allow her to explore its range fully. Again, her family guided and supported her. Whenever the Twains could scrape together a little extra money, Sharon would drive Shania south to Toronto for singing lessons. Here, in Canada's largest city, where musicians of every conceivable culture and type gravitate to music stores and studios and concert halls, a little girl from Timmins was bound to feel a bit overwhelmed and starstruck. On any given night, the city gives off its joyful noise — cool jazz, hot funk, mellifluous classical, driving rock, and soulful country — in the process entertaining thousands of discerning, music-loving natives and tourists.

The home of such legendary clubs as the Horseshoe Tavern and the Matador — where Canadian country, folk, and rock heroes from Stompin' Tom Connors and Neil Young to Prairie Oyster, Blue Rodeo, and k.d. lang captivated audiences while perfecting their craft — Toronto has long been a whistle-stop for Nashville giants. Johnny Cash, Willie Nelson, Kris Kristofferson, Alabama,

Hank Williams Jr., Garth Brooks, Dolly Parton: the list of country superstars who have made musical history at venues like the CNE Grandstand, Ontario Place, and Massey Hall is a long and impressive one. As Canada's entertainment capital, Toronto had attracted so many country musicians and fans by the late 1980s that some locals began referring to the city as Nashville North. It was only a matter of time before a rising young talent such as Shania Twain would find her way there.

The drive to Toronto from Timmins was long and tedious. Mile after mile of two-lane blacktop and rural landscape etched itself into Shania's impressionable young mind. She and Sharon would sing to pass the time, stopping occasionally at various diners and truck stops. All the while, they hoped and prayed that the truck wouldn't break down — that it would get them to where they were going just one more time. It was a lot like touring, and the experience would help to prepare Shania for those rigors of the road she would encounter later in life.

Shania endured the travel. She overcame that lost, intimidated sensation the big city triggered in her. Training hard, she set about promoting herself as an up-and-comer in the small world of Canadian country music. Vocal coaching helped her achieve the kind of range and control that is such an impressive feature of all the music she's recorded to date. Soon, her voice became her main instrument. This is not to say, however, that her love for the guitar diminished: Shania still cherished the solitude and contentment she could find locked away with her six-string. It's just that she was now spending more time working on her voice, and, like many other country performers — Nashville is packed with them — she was developing into a singer-songwriter.

Her vocal talents burgeoned, but her development as a guitar player wasn't arrested — it just didn't keep pace. Though Shania is not, obviously, a guitar virtuoso, she's a competent player. Comfortable with the instrument, she acknowledges how important it is to her, but downplays her abilities: "I'm not a great guitar player," she concedes. "I never spent very much time perfecting my skills on guitar . . . I'm a singer-songwriter." Her ax has become a primarily practical tool: "I use my guitar as an instrument to write." She admits that at one time she used the instrument as a buffer; as a very young performer, she relied on the guitar to provide her with a layer of protection. "I never performed without my guitar until I was at least sixteen," she explains. "And when I first put it down, it was so awkward without it." Still, she believes that the acoustic-guitar sound will always play an important role in her professional and personal life: "I think any singer-songwriter is comfortable doing an acoustic-type thing. They are used to just sitting and singing with the guitar. It is one of my favorite things to do" (Brown).

Shania's trademark Ovation has taken on the dimensions of a good friend. She is clearly, as many of the songs on *The Woman in Me* attest, both extremely familiar with, and adept at harmonizing to, the sounds of a lone guitar. Listen to the way her voice makes the lyrics meld with the infectious guitar riffs of "(If You're Not in It for Love) I'm Outta Here"; the song is at once reminiscent of Bobby Gentry, Robert Palmer, Nick Lowe, and Pat Benetar, and, exploiting both voice and guitar, Shania has applied a bluesy, rocking, New Wave edge to its intrinsic country feel. Then there's "No One Needs to Know" — here her vocal twang and modulations complement the acoustic so perfectly that even Hank Williams would be proud.

All through her daughter's teenage years, Sharon would also enter Shania in talent contests across Ontario; ironically, Shania never actually came in first in her home province. "You know, it's funny," she can now laugh, "but I never won a talent contest in Ontario. Mom was so discouraged. She couldn't understand why her little girl was never able to win a contest. She always came away disappointed. Then, when I was still in my early teens, Mom took me out to British Columbia to enter me in a contest there. I won in three separate categories of the contest. It was wonderful . . . and it sure made Mom happy" (Delaney, "What Made Her").

Before she had ventured very far into her teens, Shania had added numerous TV appearances to her list of credits; some Canadian viewers might even remember her lighting up the screen on programs such as *Opry North, Easy Country, The Mercey Brothers Show*, and *The Tommy Hunter Show*. These appearances, however, didn't translate into fame. Purveyors of lightweight, family-oriented entertainment, such musical variety shows exposed Shania to a large number of people, but they did not make her a household name. Shania's memories of doing the shows are still consistently happy ones, though. She remains especially fond of Hunter, a Canadian country legend. "He was such a tall man and he stood over me like a big tree. He was such a nice and friendly man — he kept telling me . . . not to be nervous about being in front of the TV cameras" (Delaney, "What Made Her"). It seems that she took Hunter's advice to heart.

These television appearances allowed her to meet a few of American country's biggest names, and from the way she talks about them, it's clear the experience was inspirational. "I remember appearing on [Hunter's] show when Ronnie Milsap was the headliner one time," she says. "And Glen Campbell headlined on another show I taped. I can remember singing 'Walk on By.' Boy, would I ever like to see tapes of those shows again!" (Delaney, "What Made Her"). Despite the pleasure such gigs brought her, it was always apparent that her music of choice just didn't have the broad appeal or marketing potential of contemporary pop and rock. Still, Shania kept picking and singing, perfecting her craft, entertaining and impressing a number of harsh judges along the way. Her voice began to blossom; it got bigger, stronger, more clearly and uniquely her own.

The "stage parent" issue has a way of creeping into any recollection of Shania's early years. It just won't be laid to rest. The interest Jerry and, especially, Sharon demonstrated in Shania's creative endeavors clearly went far beyond simple indulgence: the couple pushed, cajoled, orchestrated, and directed their daughter's life. To some extent, the Twains' dreams were riding on Shania. She confides, "My mother lived for my career. We were extremely poor . . . and she was often depressed, with five children and no food to feed them. She knew I was talented and she lived with the hope that my abilities were my chance to do something special" (Cohen).

Before she hit her teens, Shania had been obliged to accept the weight of her entire family's hopes. Whether she liked it or not, she would have to become the performer Sharon and Jerry longed for her to be. The Barbie dolls, the Easy-Bake ovens, the gymnastics evaporated in the face of their powerful dream: there would be little left to mark Shania's childhood and adolescence as typical or normal. "Coming from a poor family," she remarks, "the only thing that's going to get your children anywhere is to just push like hell. And that's what my mother did" (Jennings). The crucial distinction to make, though, is that despite their determination Jerry and Sharon were not, like so many other parents of child performers, obsessed with the seductive specter of stardom to the point of sacrificing their daughter's well-being.

For many years, the sports and entertainment industries have systematically buried and denied terrible secrets — accounts of the psychological and physical torment inflicted upon prodigies by their families and handlers were hidden from adoring fans. In the late seventies and early eighties, these repellent truths began to surface: the treatment of child stars was scrutinized both in the tabloids and in the courts. A new understanding of the raw greed and the economic machinery fueling the promotion of young talent created public awareness of the stage-parent syndrome. The problem was exposed to the light of day; the healing process began; people became complacent.

In recent years, the tide has turned again. There has been a fresh spate of child-star tell-all bios. The JonBenet Ramsay murder case has horrified millions. The figure of the stage parent has been demonized all over again. Widely published photographs of tiny beauty queen Jon-Benet, her childish features obscured behind a mask of supermodel makeup, are deeply disturbing. She seems unreal, a fabrication, a frozen symbol of neutered innocence. Controversy swirls around her family, and allegations of their involvement in her death persist. As long as child performers are treated as commodities — neat little tickets to fame and fortune — by parents who have betrayed their trust, there will be similar tragedies.

Jerry and Sharon, however, always managed to temper their proud drive with love and compassion. They ultimately demonstrated a genuine respect for Shania's individuality and a concern for her welfare. Shania continues to be questioned about her early career by skeptical interviewers who intimate that her parents went too far. She wavers, at times, in her conviction that she was happy with all the attention, and it's clear she has some mixed feelings about how much a talented youngster should be compelled to bear. So, although her parents "didn't have to force me to write songs or to be with my guitar," she felt the pressure in other ways. "The career aspect of it wasn't necessarily what I wanted. I didn't want to take it that seriously. I enjoyed being creative and doing it for myself. It's like someone saying, 'You sound great in the shower, you mind if we bring an audience tomorrow?' No, not really!" (Cohen).

It was Jerry, in the end, on whom Shania could rely when it was time to pull in the reins. Her father never forgot that Shania was, first and foremost, a child, and that the career path she was on was inherently treacherous. He wanted nothing for his daughter that she herself didn't want; this meant that he dared to dream, yet he always kept the needs of his entire family in focus. On more than one occasion, therefore, he was forced to play the heavy: saying "no" to Shania — and to Sharon, who was more prone than he to overzealousness — when the family just couldn't afford to promote her career was often his unpleasant duty.

Late one night, when Shania was still very young, Jerry again found himself cast in the heavy role, and the resulting conflict played itself out like a sitcom script. Jerry had nixed a plan they had been hatching earlier in the evening, and so Sharon and Shania conspired to make alternate, and secret, arrangements. In their eyes, Jerry was merely being stubborn. Shania remembers: "My father decided we couldn't afford to travel to a certain town to perform. After I went to bed that night, I snuck out of my window, and my mom and I went anyway." Of course,

*"Eileen" Twain,
from the 1982–83
Timmins High
and Vocational
School yearbook*

COURTESY DEBBIE
M. O'BRIEN SIRARD

Jerry just shook his head and forgave the transgression after some minor grumbling. "My father was more practical," is the way Shania explains it. "He made decisions about whether it made sense to drive somewhere to perform for free or pay the heating bill that week" (Hager).

Despite the long hours, the hard work, and the modest success she achieved as a child performer, Shania was fortunate enough to avoid peaking too soon. She didn't have to experience the kind of flash-in-the-pan, bubblegum adulation that some other young performers have endured. Being spared Debbie Gibson's fate of plummeting from child-star status straight into the where-are-they-now category, or Alanis Morissette's struggle to regain credibility as an adult artist by laboriously remaking her pop-princess image from the ground up, was a blessing in disguise.

Nashville is a beacon, drawing talent like moths. It often crushes young entertainers before they ever have the opportunity to spread their wings. That Shania was essentially crush-proof by the time she got there is testament not only to her exceptional talent, but also to the impulses and intuitions of her "stage parents." They may have pushed hard, but they took care to ensure that Shania didn't peak and fade too soon. Sharon and Jerry kept all of Shania's support structures intact and insisted that she learn to walk before she began to run — and then fly.

3

NO ONE NEEDS
TO KNOW

Pasta dishes and desserts — all kinds, but peach pie gets special mention — are the foods she loves best. At the end of 1995, Shania granted a major, comprehensive interview to *Homemaker's Magazine* that began with an anecdote about the Christmas dinner she was planning to prepare for herself and her husband. It was a perfect way to begin a magazine piece meant to cap and celebrate a marvelous year. *The Woman in Me* was selling like hotcakes, almost three million copies worldwide, and both the album and its singles dominated the *Billboard* charts. Shania was music's — not just country's — fastest-rising star. A Christmas-through–New Year holiday spent relaxing at home with her man was to be her dessert. She was on top. She had rapidly acquired all the trappings of success. *Homemaker's* interviewer John Keyes set the scene like this:

This Christmas, the woman once known as Eileen Twain will hunker down with her husband, Robert John Lange, in front of the fireplace in their studio apartment — and count her blessings.

Mind you, this isn't your average studio apartment. It's a recording studio, and the apartment area is where musicians will stay once the Big House is built. . . . Shania . . . as the new queen of country music calls herself now, and Mutt, as her husband-producer has been nicknamed since childhood, might go exploring their new 3,000-acre spread on horseback, or else just horse around with Mocha and Chocko, their two brown year-and-a-half-old Newfoundland dogs. For Christmas dinner, Twain says, she'll probably make a favourite dish, a phyllo pastry casserole with ricotta, spinach and turkey, plus sweet potatoes and cranberry sauce.

Domestic bliss. Even though her professional life had reached a fever pitch, Shania still found time to turn her own much-needed spell of downtime into a small Christmas present for her fans. This interview gave them a little bit more of Shania; it allowed them a glimpse of who she really is and how she wants to live. Secluded, productive, quiet, contemplative, happy . . . and well fed. Giving and taking, that's what it's all about.

So much has been made about how she often went hungry as a little girl that it's not surprising Shania is frequently drawn into discussions about food. Embarrassed that the Twains' poverty was often so severe that they were unable to eat regularly, Shania now takes pride in being a relatively lavish provider. Cooking, it seems, is not only a favorite hobby — it's therapy. Whipping up creative meals to share with her friends and family, she buries those unpleasant memories of a grumbling stomach and mustard sandwiches. Now she can afford anything her heart desires, but those flashbacks of abject poverty still haunt her. They affect the way she lives her life. Accordingly, there's nothing excessive about Shania; she refuses to flaunt her newfound wealth.

This Christmas-dinner scene is typical: food for Shania is reassurance. Having enough to eat means that everything is all right in her world. "I love to cook," she declares. "I like to get up in the morning and put a stew on or put soup on . . . go play with the dogs, go to the stable, clean the stalls, brush them down . . . go for walks. I like to snowmobile. I love sitting by the fire and reading. I'm just a very average, pretty square person" (Phillips). Simple things, everyday chores and activities, put her life into perspective.

In hindsight the Twain-Lange 1995 Christmas dinner, as presented in the Keyes interview, actually seems a bit too perfect — a nouvelle-cuisine repast with just the right touch of tradition. The food works as a neat metaphor for the star herself: a down-home girl (turkey, sweet potatoes, cranberry sauce) with just enough intriguing exoticism (phyllo, ricotta) to elevate her out of the mundane. Everybody can relate to that. The mechanisms of promotion are geared to make their celebrity object seem accessible; the celebrity is, in effect, packaged to appear more like her fans. Consider this: in May of 1996, just six months later, *Chatelaine* reported that Shania had been a "vegetarian for two years" (Schneller). So what was the turkey doing on the Yuletide table? Of course, there are a number of plausible answers to this question, but the point is that the publicity machine had already kicked in, and the real Shania had begun to disappear behind such elaborately constructed public-private banquets as that of Christmas 1995.

So many reporters, promotion people, and fans have been caught up with the idea of Shania, what she represents, that they've often taken liberties in interpreting her.

At times, she's been snowed under by the avalanche of what's been written and said. After *The Woman in Me*, her life was placed under a microscope. Everybody wanted a piece of her heartwarming, compelling biography. People started emerging from her past to add to the mythology, and every bit of information spawned a new tale. Interviewers and commentators became so obsessed with finding the freshest angle that the facts were often distorted to fit their prefabricated story lines. Shania just couldn't keep up. Unable to clarify everything the media was spouting about her, she resigned herself to doing the best she could, and so now that the two-and-a-half-year media blitz has subsided, some contradictions have become entrenched.

Yes, Shania is a vegetarian, and depending on how you look at it, considering her heritage and her history, that's either perfectly understandable or somewhat strange. And yes, knowing Shania, she would prepare a traditional dinner for someone she loved that included meat. That kind of generosity is clearly part of her nature. But what's important is that the Keyes interview was as much about presenting an entertaining yarn as it was about getting at the truth. The fact is, most of what was written about Shania during her rise to stardom was not hard journalism. Much of it wasn't even concerned with *The Woman in Me* or Shania's talent as a musician. Instead, the hype was a manifestation of our society's thriving cult of personality. The media sought out and reported the feel-good story; it was soft journalism all the way; a lot of Shania's early press was focused solely on either her beauty or the rags-to-riches aspect of her ascent. The music itself was hardly ever discussed.

With so many pieces of her life floating around in blips and sound bites, it's not surprising that things sometimes become confused. Furthermore, such fragmentation has made Shania more vulnerable to attack. Laurence Leamer, in his book *Three Chords and the Truth*, an insider's look at the American country-music industry, goes so far as to accuse her of flagrant dissimulation. Leamer identifies discrepancies in media depictions of her life as evidence of well-orchestrated manipulation. Laboring under the assumption that Shania has conned the public in order to further her career, he dismisses her, arguing that she hasn't been true to the roots of country.

In reality, though, Shania's only crime is that she's had the unmitigated gall to attain success in a way that's not recognized by Nashville's old guard. Her whole career has been about breaking down barriers and jettisoning the tired old conventions that have dictated what a country musician is permitted to do. By blurring the distinctions between pop, rock, and country, both musically and in terms of marketing, Shania has taken the Nashville establishment to places it never dreamed of visiting. People like Leamer are afraid of her. Afraid of the possibilities she represents. They want Nashville to circle the wagons.

Their fear is a token of her success, and success of this kind and magnitude, in our time, is a product of publicity. On CTV television's *W5*, Dave Hartt, a Timmins record-store employee who is also a keyboardist/singer/songwriter, talked about how he played with Shania in one of her first teenage bands. He half-jokingly referred to Shania as a beautiful "package." And while he caught himself up, and then quickly acknowledged that she's much more than that, his terminology is significant ("Gold Country"). As an icon, Shania *has* become a package: as with any other celebrity, her fame derives in part from the fact that she looks and acts the part.

During a dinner break in Manhattan, while shooting

the video for "(If You're Not in It for Love) I'm Outta Here," Shania took a plate of rice, only rice, back to her trailer. It was just one of the occasional sacrifices she's had to make in order to maintain her image. A svelte body is integral to the package her fans expect her to maintain. After all, she has to fit into the clothes they expect her to wear. But such moderation is also a response to her childhood: "If I ever get fat because I eat too much, I couldn't be satisfied with myself," she candidly reveals. "Because I would think, 'There's extra pounds on me, and there's kids out there that . . .' I sure could have left a little, and not consumed it myself. When I make dinner, I'm perfect at just making enough. My husband says, 'What are you trying to do, starve me?' But it's the mind-set of my childhood, the grooves that end up in your brain" (Schneller).

Hunger, for those who have seen or felt it, can become an obsession. And Shania evokes it and its antidote — food — as emblems of her past. A longing to be filled, fulfilled, has become an element of her character. That element is a destructive experience transformed into a productive impulse: ambition. A remarkable drive is what now burns in the pit of Shania's stomach, and work is the only thing that satiates her. She does what she does because she's consumed by a creative hunger. She needs to be unique, and her boundless, carefully directed energy makes that uniqueness possible. Shania's vegetarianism is just one more aspect of her difference. In the meat-and-potatoes world of traditional country music, she's both a prodigal daughter and a perennial outsider.

Reconciling contradictions such as these is imperative if you want to glimpse Shania unadorned and unaltered. You have to seek out the solutions to what seem like simple puzzles. What makes a young Native woman, who at one time hunted and killed her own food, become a vegetarian? Find the answers and you've found the real Shania Twain. To do so, you must go back to the days when there was no Shania, just Eileen. Back to the days when Jerry grounded her life.

Jerry was a hardworking outdoorsman who loved the land. He prided himself on being able to infuse his family with Ojibwa values and traditions while he labored to put food on the table. He gave of himself so that his children would have the chance to discover who they were. Shania remembers: "We camped out a lot when I was growing up. . . . Not in campgrounds, but out in the bush, or near an uninhabited lake my father knew about.

Eileen Twain with high-school friend Debbie O'Brien Sirard in Niagara Falls, Ontario, 1984
COURTESY DEBBIE M. O'BRIEN SIRARD

We would just sleep in the back of the truck or pitch a canvas tent somewhere" (Hager). This experience brought her closer to Jerry and to the rest of her family. It also fostered in her a special affinity for her wilderness surroundings. And so Shania's need for solitude, and her love for Canada's North, came to her through Jerry.

Every story ever reported by Shania is in some sense informed by Jerry's everlasting influence. Having Jerry Twain as a father made Shania unique before her career ever took off. "People can't believe the bush stories," she remarks. "I guess the American way would be cowboys, while where I was raised it was more of a wilderness situation. A lot of people were curious." At the 1994 Nashville Fan Fair, she says, her booth "was packed" with fans who wanted to know more about where she was from (Chodan, "Twain Goes"). The cover of her self-titled first album had piqued their interest. Artwork for *Shania Twain* features her standing with a trained wolf named Cane, wrapped in a deerskin jacket, and wearing fur-lined mukluks. A fire blazes, creating an atmospheric glow around her tightly bundled form. Blue light radiates from the snow-covered Timmins field behind her. Juxtaposed with the imposing animal (shipped in from Vancouver for the occasion), the young singer looks both sexy and mysterious. Still, there is something surreal about it all — it has the distinct feel of an alien landscape. Shania, ever the proud northern girl, borrowed her grandfather's snowshoes to scout the location herself. She was going to leave nothing to chance.

It's easy for Shania to talk about this part of her life. Her northern experience is always with her, making her alternately homesick and secure in her identity, informing her art. The old cliché applies readily to Shania: you can take the girl out of the country, but you can't take the country out of the girl. When she was not going to school, practicing and playing music, or working, she spent days and nights in the great outdoors. Her father used the bush as a vast schoolroom: the lessons he offered there taught Shania and her siblings about the nature of happiness, their heritage, and the value of all forms of life. All of the Twain children, boys or girls, were equals in Jerry's mind; if Shania, or Jill, or Carrie-Ann were willing to enter the bush and learn, he'd teach them a thing or two about their country.

The bottom line, however, was that living off the land was a necessary part of the Twains' routine. Money was so tight that a sufficient amount of store-bought food was frequently beyond their reach. The fruits of Jerry's hunting, trapping, and fishing expeditions were a vital supplement to his family's diet. He and his father, Shania's grandfather, worked traplines, and eventually everybody in the family was expected to hunt when necessary. Shania has been mocked for her stories about eating moose and rabbit; these tales, though, are true, and the ridicule of those who have never had to worry about where their next meal is coming from is unwarranted.

"My father taught us to kill our own food," Shania recalls, "and my job was to set the rabbit snares. It looks like a guitar string that you rig up in a loop. When the rabbit gives a little tug, it's strangled" ("Shania Snares"). This may seem brutal, even eccentric, to many people — it's easy to settle into the vague notion that our meat comes from a supermarket cooler, that it came into being sitting on a Styrofoam tray sealed in plastic wrap, neatly formed into a favorite cut. Yet beautiful Shania, who today looks like she could never have harmed a fly, and who is, by choice, a vegetarian, "killed her own food" because she hadn't the luxury of choosing not to. And so why hide it?

She boasts, "I'm also good with a gun"; "It was nothing for me to shoot partridge" (Leamer; "Gold Country"). Hunger breeds practicality. Shania couldn't afford to be squeamish.

While learning to hunt, Shania also learned from Jerry never to squander the lives of her prey. As soon as she was able to understand, her father impressed on her that the natural world and its creatures were sacred. He would simply not tolerate their abuse. Neither would Shania. At a very early age, she developed a deep affection for animals — her special affinity for dogs and horses is now obvious. In the first three *The Woman in Me* videos, she can be seen ruffling the fur on a dog's head, heading off to muck out a horse's stall, and riding like a pro. She's completely at ease, interacting naturally with each member of her supporting cast. In fact, the viewer is left with the sense that she's more relaxed *because* these animals are present. Riding a horse through the acres of wilderness that surround her New York State home is one of her preferred relaxation techniques.

Recently, the newest addition to her cherished canine family has become Shania's regular traveling companion. Her career demands that she take to the road on average three weeks out of four, and Mutt, who's happiest out of the spotlight, often remains at home. After all, as a top record producer, his schedule can be as hectic as his spouse's. So Shania's traveling companion is a loyal German shepherd named Tim, whose name serves as a constant reminder to Shania of Timmins — her home, her past, a marker of the great distance she has come. Trained to protect his mistress, Tim gives Shania a sense of security and a certain freedom. This service is invaluable to anyone in the throes of celebrity, and Shania knows it. Her fame, she acknowledges, has forced her to rethink what she calls

"Eileen" Twain, 1984
BARB BLANCHARD/DAN PORTER, COURTESY *COUNTRY MUSIC NEWS*

her "control-freak" tendencies, her compulsion to do for herself, and she realizes she can't enjoy the kind of independence she once took for granted. "I knew that success would mean change," she says. "And I'm enjoying it. But I'm also going through the most dependent period of my life. Even as a child I was more independent. That's why I got my dog Tim" (Hager).

More than a bodyguard, Tim is a stabilizing influence, one antidote for the stresses of Shania's life. It's typical of Shania to seek comfort and companionship in a member of the animal kingdom. "I really love animals, and I become quite excited and childlike around them," she has written. "Even watching them from a distance is extremely pleasurable to me" ("Fan Letter" 1994). In fact, if she hadn't fulfilled her dreams of becoming a singer, she would have become a veterinarian. She occasionally jokes about giving up her illustrious music career to do just that. This desire to be closer to the animal and natural worlds actually says a great deal about Shania. "I love escaping the prison of beauty and vanity — not curling my eyelashes and [wearing] lipstick, just throwing on a hat and a coat that doesn't match and a pair of funky boots [to] go out and play with the animals" ("Shania Twain Has a Plan B"). Shania still loves the things she loved best when she was young Eileen. Some things never change.

Those passions came into play in an extremely practical way when Jerry and Sharon started their own reforestation business. Teenaged Shania became fully involved. It was tough work. Jerry organized teams to revive forests that had been stripped or depleted by the logging industry. Shania learned all about axes and chain saws, seedlings and soil, and soon she was supervising her own crew. Though still at an age when most young women are preoccupied with friends, hanging out, and boys, Shania found herself in charge of up to thirteen workers. Most of these were older Cree and Ojibwa people from northern Ontario communities such as Moosonee, Moose Factory, and Manitoulin Island.

"It was a real family business," Shania says. "My grandparents worked in the camp kitchen, my aunt kept books back in Timmins, my mom looked after things in camp, and my father ran the forest operations" (Hager). It was backbreaking work for a girl who might otherwise have continued pulling a few shifts at McDonald's or become a sales clerk at the local mall. As a foreperson, she had to rise at dawn to prepare for the day ahead. Shania dug and planted with everyone else. And like everyone else in the camp, she had to subsist on a diet that was constituted mainly of baked beans, bread, and tea.

Still, it would be false to create the impression that Shania was totally unfamiliar with all the creature comforts of the modern world. Timmins (as well as the other small towns and cities Shania grew up in) is not an outpost in a time warp as some who have written about Shania would have us believe. You don't have to be a rugged pioneer to live there. All the amenities and entertaining nonessentials are on hand: when she had a little extra cash in her pocket, Shania went to first-run Hollywood movies and bought candy bars. She experienced the joys of indoor plumbing. Critics have suggested that Shania herself has offered inflated accounts of her deprived childhood, milking these stories in an effort to play the heartstrings of her fans and to make what she's achieved seem all the more incredible. Some have gone so far as to charge her with blatantly misinforming people about Timmins and northern Ontario. But a big part of the problem has been how misguided or romantic the media have been. Many reporters have only heard what they want to hear; some hacks never bother with original research. A vivid picture of what growing up in a community like Timmins in the 1970s or 1980s was all about is, therefore, generally missing from profiles of Shania.

Shania's portrayals *were* genuine because they faithfully reflected *her own* experience — not that of anyone else — and her upbringing was undeniably atypical. As such, it colored her response to her surroundings. Leamer again points the finger at Shania, countering that she's at fault for not going out of her way to shatter all the illusions that sprang up around her as soon as she became a public persona. He does have a point, however, when he says that "the mythic Timmins," a kind of hardscrabble backwater, "provided a perfect backdrop for the most poignant tales of poverty by a country star since the Great Depression." But Shania has made it clear, when she was not specifically describing her own circumstances, that her town was and is, in fact, a thriving and progressive community. Can anybody reasonably contend that she's to blame for articles and interviews that fail to mention this?

There are times when vocal self-defense is necessary. Shania has been too proud and too confident to respond to criticisms such as Leamer's — and such restraint, in the long run, serves her well. Her evident belief in herself gives her credibility. But you can't always just turn the other cheek, especially when your culture is under attack. In the wake of the tremendous success of *The Woman in Me*, Shania found herself embroiled in a scandal concerning the authenticity of her Native heritage. She braced herself for a war of words. Some background will help us to understand how she was backed into this particular corner.

As the public learned more about Shania, *The Woman in Me* became an even greater success. If tales of childhood poverty struck a chord in country-music fans, then stories of survival in the Canadian North captured their imaginations. Shania's beauty worked its charm; the combination of her velvet voice and sassy lyrics proved addictive; and her Native heritage imbued her with an appealing touch of exoticism. As a Native, Shania seemed so much more noble in her struggles, and her triumph appeared even sweeter. She did not exploit her origins, however. In fact, she tried to play them down. Being a Native was, for her, like being a woman — a simple fact of life.

Among all the trophies Shania has received, one of the most personally significant, and perhaps least high profile, is a First Americans in the Arts Outstanding Musical Achievement Award. Given to her in recognition of how her successes have honored her culture, the distinction serves as a lasting reminder of the community that first embraced her. Jerry Twain, a full-blooded Ojibwa, was a member of the Temagami Anishnawbe Bear Island First Nation band. His father — Shania's grandfather — spoke only Ojibwa. He, Jerry, and Shania's grandmother taught her a little bit of the language. Jerry and her grandfather instructed Shania in the fine art of tracking. By locating the point where rabbit prints intersected, she was told, you could determine where to focus your efforts. Shania paid close attention, often heading into the wilderness on her own with their lessons in mind.

Her Native family helped her to build the foundations of her music career, too. From the first, she was encouraged to approach music as part of communal experience. Jerry's family comprised Shania's initial audience, and it wasn't long after she first picked up her instrument that she was playing for them on holiday occasions, at parties, or whenever the clan got together. Some of Jerry's cousins were actually members of Shania's first impromptu "band." They'd help her through the songs, but she was almost always the center of attention. Self-esteem, support, praise: these were the gifts Shania's Native family bestowed upon her.

Sharon, in the meantime, busily managed her daughter's burgeoning career — organizing concerts at community centers, in public parks, and at clubs, booking television appearances — but Shania's favorite regular gig was at the local senior citizens' home. It wasn't just that the audiences were so receptive and appreciative. Shania loved rocking the home because her own great-grandfather Twain was a proud member of the audience. Before she could ever possibly have been aware of it, Shania's music was bridging the gap between three generations. This link to her great-grandfather in turn linked her to a history more vast than she ever imagined. Jerry retained a sense of humor about it all: Shania recalls, with one of her radiant smiles, "My dad would say I was playing both the cowboy and the Indian because I'd wear a buckskin jacket and cowboy boots" (Hager).

In the end, though, much of what Jerry Twain taught his children about their Native roots he imparted without resorting to words at all; they learned, instead, from his example. One important exception to this general rule was that he did tell his brood not to expect or seek out special treatment on the basis of their cultural differences. He believed that they should demand to be judged according to their own merits. This lesson, in particular, has shaped Shania's life and career. "My dad told us to pursue success as individuals," she says (Hager). Shania has done so fiercely, but there has been a price to pay. Jerry also made his kids understand that there would be times when they would suffer for the prejudices of others, and at a tender age Shania felt the sting of racism, the fallout of ignorance and hatred.

Sharon and Jerry made several moves in the course of Shania's childhood in order to find work. The Twains set up housekeeping not only in Timmins, but also in Sudbury and South Porcupine. Shania and her siblings were often the new kids on the block, and, if the Twains were not the only Native family in the community, then they were one of only a few. This brought them closer and forced them to rely upon one another. They stuck up for their own out of necessity — they often found themselves regarded with suspicion by other children. Shania frequently found herself championing her younger brothers and sister when the cruelty of those children — the progeny of bigoted parents — got out of hand. Her conviction grew rock solid: nobody would ever be allowed to mess with a member of her family. Period.

As she got older, her poise and self-confidence in the face of aggression grew stronger and stronger. Entering high school, she felt no lightening of the atmosphere. On several occasions it was communicated to her that the parents of friends considered her racially and culturally unacceptable. When a boyfriend's parents forbade their son to date Shania, she was deeply hurt — yet unsurprised. She absorbed the blow and carried on. It certainly wasn't the first time she'd tasted discrimination, and she knew it wouldn't be the last.

Like father, like daughter. Such early experiences would be enough to turn many a sensitive young person into a cultural militant. Not Shania. Instead, she has chosen to lead by example. Today she understands that many Native American women, young and old alike (but especially young), look to her as a role model. Their acceptance of her music has only added to her inner resources. For the sake of history and community, she declares, "it's important to be in touch with your culture" (Hager). Still, Shania has the intelligence to know that if she is to retain her artistic autonomy she cannot limit herself. It is vital that she keep her identity as a Native distinct from her identity as a performer. If she can do this, she will preserve the integrity of both. She'll also provide a bit less grist for the publicity mill that tends to churn out distortions. "I don't like to talk to the media about growing up in a Native family," she told Barbara Hager, a Native interviewer, "because people tend to romanticize it. Some people want me to have grown up with braids and feathers in my hair. My family were hardworking people from Northern Ontario. We trapped and hunted. . . . But we watched television like everyone else."

Shania's cultural heritage enhances her art as it enhances her life. It is where her unique identity begins, but not where it ends. And, as such, it is not something to exploit — it is something to protect with everything she's got. "We grew up like every other family in Canada, but there were things that made our family different from our white neighbors," Shania explains. "The typical Native family in Canada is like everyone else, except we're standing in quicksand. We're fighting to preserve and regain what's ours. But it takes generations. Even my grandparents have lost some of their traditions. But the reality of being Native in Canada is how you live your everyday life, whether that means in a traditional way, or by using your language, or simply surviving" (Hager).

When the scandal broke, Shania must have felt the irony acutely. She was accustomed to the kind of prejudice her Native origins spawned in others, but completely unprepared for the new heritage-related onslaught that rained down on her. She was suddenly in the unimaginable position of having to prove that she was both Jerry Twain's daughter and an Ojibwa. This time, however, the blame could not simply be placed on the shoulders of racist classmates or overzealous reporters on the trail of a hot story. The question of whether Shania Twain was or wasn't a "real" Native rapidly became one of the most fascinating and complex country-music stories of 1996 — the kind of item that both mainstream media outlets and the tabloids bank on. Shania, who had always been so forthcoming with journalists and fans, now had to restate, clarify, and sometimes even retract statements she had made about her identity. She had committed the sin of omission, but firmly believed her actions were justifiable. Then, as more details came to light, it became apparent that she had actually revised her true history in order to produce one she felt more comfortable with. And, as these things so regularly do, it came back to haunt her.

The source of the scandal emerged, ghostlike, from a void of almost thirty years. From out of the blue, the name Clarence Edwards hit the airwaves and news wires. Shania quickly responded by offering an eloquent defense of Jerry's paternal right: "For me to acknowledge another man as my father, who wasn't the one who struggled every day to put food on our table, would have hurt him terribly. We were a family. Step-fathers, step-brothers, we never used that vocabulary in our home. To have referred to him as my step-father would have been the worst slap across the face to him" (Bissley).

Yet soon enough, Shania was forced to acknowledge the existence of her biological father: a man whom most of the world had never even heard of. If the nature of the role Clarence Edwards played in Shania's life to this day remains unclear, then Shania herself has helped to make it so. She claimed to have barely known him: "I've never had a relationship with my biological father. Although I was briefly introduced to Clarence a couple of times in my teen years, I never knew him growing up" (Leamer). Then came reports that Shania had never met the man at all, that she knew next to nothing about him except that she had been led to believe he might have Native blood.

Months later, Shania told still another story. She characterized Edwards as a good-for-nothing drunk, and insisted that she was happy never to have met him. It's difficult to hide anything from the intruding, scrutinizing lens of the television camera, and it was plain that Shania was bone weary and very hurt by the whole sorry mess. "Clarence called a couple of times during my life," she said. "Once, after my parents died, and somewhere else in between . . . intoxicated. So I wasn't interested in knowing somebody who . . . it's like, you know, 'You're calling me now and you're not even straight?'" ("Gold Country").

But Shirley Caby, Clarence's common-law wife for over twenty-five years, blasted holes in Shania's story. Clarence and Shania saw one another on a regular basis throughout Shania's childhood, Caby asserted — at least several times a year, usually during holidays. In fact, she continued, Clarence tried to develop closer ties to all of his daughters; he wanted to expand the scope of his relationship with Shania long before she became a country-music celebrity. The Twains, however, in Caby's opinion, eventually managed to push Clarence Edwards away (Leamer).

The *Timmins Daily Press* initially broke the story. Its readership was enthralled: was one of Canada's favorite daughters, like disgraced Olympic gold-medal sprinter Ben Johnson, destined to become a fallen angel? Was she, of all things, a liar? The mainstream national entertainment news media in Toronto and Vancouver picked it up. Then the Canadian music industry was abuzz: for weeks, conflicting opinions were bandied about over morning coffee, through lunch, until long past quitting time. In the meantime — it was inevitable — Nashville devoured the juicy bit of intrigue.

Shania felt betrayed by her hometown paper. They had enjoyed a long, equitable, productive relationship, and in the end it had come to this. The *Daily Press* had been the first publication to recognize and promote Shania's talent. It had pronounced her a prodigy, a young woman Timmins should feel proud to claim as its own. Later, the paper issued regular reports about her exploits, and Shania, in turn, after she'd entered the major leagues, never forgot how good the *Daily Press* had been to her. No matter how hectic things got, she'd always try to make herself available to its reporters. Abruptly, two months before the April 1996 Nashville Fan Fair, that bond was shattered. "The Father Shania Turned Her Back On," "Grandma [Edwards's mother] Waits for Call," "Shania Confesses She Might Not Be Native," the *Daily Press* blared. And Shania was stunned. Every star knows that the odds of being skewered by the tabloids at least once during his or her career are high. It's practically a ritual of initiation. Never, though, did Shania intuit that the heat source would be her own hometown rag. Never did she anticipate that the Canadian media in general would ever be so vicious.

This is how it happened. Two *Daily Press* reporters, Brad Hunter and Dawn Liersch, received a tip that Shania was not everything she claimed to be. An unidentified caller contacted the paper and urged Hunter and Liersch to question the authenticity of Shania's Native heritage. They'd find the star was lying, the caller assured them.

Shania Twain did not have a drop of Native blood in her veins. The reporters quickly found their way to Clarence Edwards and to his mother, Shania's biological grandmother, eighty-five-year-old Regina Nutbrown. She confirmed the caller's accusation. The resulting front-page article, the piece that altered Shania's public life forever, read: ". . . Twain has woven a tapestry of half-truths and outright lies in her climb to the top of the country charts" (Leamer). John Farrington, the *Daily Press*'s publisher, defended his decision to run this first story and those that followed it in rapid succession by insisting that Shania had brought it all upon herself: "I think that she didn't mention her full background because it didn't fit the story . . . never once was the adoption part of her life ever mentioned" ("Gold Country").

To his credit, Edwards refused to comment. He chose to remain silent, despite the fact that his own identity and heritage were being called into question. Sharon, Shania knew, had been of Irish descent. She had told her daughters, however, that there was some Native blood in Clarence Edwards's family. Shania had no reason to doubt the veracity of this information. The combination of this element of her biological heritage and the already established fact of her Native, Twain-derived cultural heritage, she argued, justified her claim to a Native identity. Shania's step-aunt, Karen Twain, corroborated Shania's claim. Sharon, she reported, on more than one occasion had remarked that her first husband had also had Native blood. But the Edwards family, through Regina Nutbrown and other spokespeople, adamantly denied any Native connection: they were of French Irish stock, and nobody could prove otherwise (Bissley).

Shania had hit a brick wall. She decided to issue an official statement defending her own integrity. It was both succinct and defiant, because she had not, in her own mind, done anything wrong. "I don't know how much Indian blood I actually have in me," she confessed, "but as the adopted daughter of my father Jerry, I became legally registered as 50 percent North American Indian. Being raised by a full-blooded Indian and being part of his family and their culture from such a young age is all I've ever known. The heritage is in my heart and soul, and I'm proud of it" ("Twain Not Truthful"). This is absolutely reasonable. Only the truly mean-spirited could find fault with it. The fault lies in what the statement *doesn't* say.

Why did Shania lie Clarence Edwards out of existence? To further her career? To give Jerry Twain the full measure of credit for her upbringing? To shield a corner of her past from the public gaze — a corner that to her was of minor importance and that would be accorded a greater significance than it deserved if it was revealed? Even before all the songs for *The Woman in Me* had been written and recorded, Shania had made the decision to lie. As early as May of 1994, while still promoting *Shania Twain*, she wrote, "I am the only child in our family who wasn't actually born in Timmins — my mother was out of town on a visit to Windsor when I was born in 1965." This fabrication is not a response to a reporter's question, and that, in a sense, makes her actions all the more damning. It was offered up in the context of "the first fan letter I've ever written to the public," a kind of thank-you note to her loyal supporters. "[H]opefully," comments Shania, apparently without a trace of irony, "you will read things in this . . . that you have never read before" ("Fan Letter" 1994).

And she persisted. As 1995 drew to a close and Shania could feel secure that her good fortune would endure —

RACHELE LABRECQUE

The Woman in Me was a monster hit; she'd garnered five Canadian Country Music Awards and appeared on both Jay Leno's and David Letterman's late-night, high-powered self-promotion fests — she confidently told interviewer John Keyes that Jerry Twain was her father. Five months later, the scandal broke. The Keyes interview may have been one of her final opportunities to come clean before it was too late. But maybe even then the web she'd created had become too tangled.

Regina Nutbrown did most of the talking for the Edwards family. She said they felt betrayed, insulted, and neglected: "All she talks about is this Indian man, but what about her real father? What about us? I wrote her about a year ago but once she started going good she never wrote. I wish she would. I don't know what's happened to her" ("Country Singer"). And no, Nutbrown remarked, she wasn't surprised that the truth had been brought to light when it had, though she denied the suggestion that the Edwards family had tipped off the press out of spite. "I guess somebody in town got angry seeing Eileen on television pretending we don't exist," she told reporters from her home in Chapleau, a small northern lumber community 120 miles west of Timmins ("Twain Not Truthful"). Suddenly, Nutbrown was re-created in the media as the lonely and forgotten granny of a cold-hearted new star.

The Twain family, of course, rallied around their pride and joy. Shania's beloved step-grandmother was deeply distressed by the uproar, but too ill to comment. Willis McKay, Jerry Twain's first cousin, came forward to put the family position into perspective. "Speaking as a Native person," he said from his home on the Temagami reserve, "we treated [Shania] as Native, raised her as Native. We accepted her as part of our family, no questions asked." The rest of the world should do the same. "Three years ago," he continued, "when the first album came out, she did a big concert here in Timmins. Everyone from the reserve went and most of the people from town were there. She brought her [Twain] grandmother on stage and acknowledged us as her family. Nobody said anything then" (Bissley).

When Shania was offered her first Nashville recording contract, she had to apply for American immigration status. Because Jerry Twain was a full-blooded Ojibwa who enjoyed all "the rights guaranteed to Native Americans in the Jay Treaty" of 1794, Shania was legally registered in the course of that application as having fifty percent

Native blood (Bissley). There was no deception here: Shania is, in the eyes of both Canadian and American law, a Native. The controversy over her heritage clearly had no legal basis. It was generated, instead, by the thorny issue of personal ethics. And in the Native community, it took on a greater, universal dimension: Shania Twain is Native, beyond a doubt, so how, then, do we define what constitutes "Native identity" in the modern world? Barbara Hager, the author of *Honour Song*, a collection of interviews with and testimonials by prominent Canadian Natives (including Shania herself), supports Shania's claim to her heritage. Comments Hager: "Native identity is not about DNA tests. . . . Shania grew up as a Native kid in a Native environment. That's what matters" (Goyette).

Most — though not all — Native commentators share Hager's perspective on Shania. All, however, concur that the issue of whether Shania or any other individual is Native should be determined by First Nations communities, and certainly not by the white media. It is sad that Shania's ordeal has ultimately come to serve as an object lesson for the Native community at large. As writer Jackie Bissley points out, Shania is just one of many who, "as children and now as adults, find themselves caught in a crossfire between the political and social exercise of nation building and the legacy of the Indian act."

In hiding the true story of her birth, Shania not only disappointed her fans, exposed her private life to the worst kind of scrutiny, and dented her professional image, but also placed herself in the center of an ongoing political battle of much larger proportions. It didn't take her very long to recognize that this new, and vulnerable, position would call for a new mind-set. The woman who said, "I care passionately about many issues, including Native American rights, but I don't believe that my

opinion should be any more valid than anybody else's. . . .
Why should things change just because Shania Twain gets
up and says they should?" (Richmond), would also have
to address the bigger picture. "I have never played an
active role in the larger Native community, just my own
Native family, that's all I've ever known. My success as a
country singer has brought me into that larger community. I'm aware of that now. The most important thing
to me is that the community, especially the Native youth,
understand that I have not lied to them," she declared —
and then the pain and defiance flared again: "This is
tearing me apart from my family — robbing me of
my identity and I won't let anyone do that to me or my
family" (Bissley).

The war continued to rage on a number of fronts.
Shania's management team climbed into the trenches and
began to lob some legal grenades, using the *Daily Press* of
Timmins as its target. The paper found itself threatened
with a major lawsuit and saw its contract to print Shania's
letters to her fanclub canceled. Leamer contends that it
was a clear case of overkill. The *Daily Press*, he says, "pulled
at one single strand of Shania's story and her lawyers and
publicists reacted as if the whole mythic image of Shania
risked unravelling."

Finally, after an involved and somewhat bitter negoti-
ation process, the *Daily Press* and Shania settled. The paper
published an apology in the form of a "clarification."
"The Daily Press," the notice read, "accepts Ms. Twain's
statement that there is a widely shared misunderstanding
about the identity of Ms. Twain's natural father. . . . The
Daily Press sincerely regrets any suggestion that Ms. Twain
lied" (Leamer). The point that many people, including
Leamer, missed, however, was that in Shania's mind all of
this had very little to do with her career. It was personal.

The fact that the paper had turned on her hurt her deeply, where she lived, and had caused her family to suffer. It was so hard to get past that, and she couldn't do it without a fight.

By running that clarification, the *Daily Press* effectively marked the conclusion of the saga. For all intents and purposes, the nature of Shania's heritage had become a dead issue. Still, Shania is occasionally pestered by reporters who refuse to let it drop from sight. And her reputation within the entertainment industry — and particularly among country-music insiders — continues to bear the taint. She still fields the annoying questions, but she's understandably more careful in her replies, all the while insisting that it's water under the bridge. "[T]hat kind of attention from the media is inevitable. I didn't let it get to me," she maintains, sounding as though she's trying hard to convince herself (Richmond).

And, in the final analysis, what about the fans? The Native community? How has the scandal affected the way Shania is perceived in these quarters? At a glance, the answer would seem to be a simple one: it hasn't. If Shania ever really slid, during all of this, in the public's estimation, then she's bounced right back. *The Woman in Me* benefited from the publicity. Record sales continued strong through 1996. Increased public awareness of her meant a reinforcement of her celebrity status, which in turn meant that more people, and people from diverse backgrounds, became interested in her music. And once they got a listen — radio and video programmers, listeners and viewers alike — they were hooked.

Shania crossed over, and was no longer just a country sensation. The scandal, in fact, even led to her acting debut. In mid-April 1996, millions of American and Canadian viewers had the opportunity to get a glimpse of the star everybody was talking about when she appeared on *Saturday Night Live* as part of a David Spade skit. She defended herself against the allegations that she had misrepresented her heritage with poise and self-deprecating wit.

★ ★ ★

If you look at photos of Sharon and Jerry Twain together, two things become crystal clear: they were a handsome couple, and they came from very different cultures. Jerry's dark complexion and striking features complement Sharon's quiet, fair beauty. Then watch as those glamorous video images of Shania flicker past. Scan her glossy publicity stills. What you see is a stunning, vivacious young woman. But what don't you see? In a word, her heritage. Shania is white. This single visual indicator of an entire world of racial and cultural distinctions — skin color — that would link her at a glance to Jerry, and through him to the Ojibwa nation, simply isn't there. But just because Shania's Native identity can't be captured on film doesn't mean it's not a real force in her life, informing everything she does. Shania is Native. Take it or leave it. Deal with it.

Family snapshots of Shania — still Eileen — taken in the late 1980s while she was busy raising her young brothers reveal how palpable the issue of race and identity must have been to them all. Again, notice the contrast. Shania is thin, pale complexioned, tough, responsible, adult. Darryl and Mark are lean as well. In the full bloom of their adolescence, they are tall, dark, and handsome — clearly half-Native — and obviously their father's sons. The physical badge of their heritage indicates that they have had to deal with their ancestry in a way that Shania has never been compelled to do. The very color of her brothers' skin announces: "I'm Native. Take it or leave it."

Of course, Shania understands this. So when she uttered those words to a reporter backstage after the 1997 Juno Awards, and anytime she publicly proclaims her Native identity, she was and is expressing solidarity with her brothers, her family, her entire culture. When she tells someone to "deal with" her heritage, she is not only speaking for herself. She is also representing all the Twains, no matter how much Native blood they have. She is, in effect, speaking as a representative of all First Nations people. And she knows her celebrity will ensure that her voice is heard.

4

YOU WIN MY LOVE

It was one hell of a year. A series of highs, a chain of celebrations and triumphs. For Shania and the Canadian country-music industry — for the Canadian music industry in general — the momentum never seemed to falter: 1995 was sheer platinum.

In February, *The Woman in Me* was released, but at first sales were only moderate. Early reviews were mixed, but a number of them noted Shania's potential. The uniqueness of the album's sound and production values were almost always mentioned. This record, most critics were saying, was different. Gradually, marketing and promotional efforts began to bear fruit. The album started to attract the attention of all the right people. Slick, spunky, and supersexy videos produced to accompany the disc actually unsettled some industry types: Shania had gone too far; all this flash and sex was too much for the relatively staid country market.

The fans, however, did not agree. Shania's videos proved their mass appeal; her audience demonstrated that it was more liberal and more mature than Nashville industry brass had ever imagined. After all, habitual video viewers were accustomed to a steady diet of sex and glitz — MTV is one big clamor for instant attention — and they knew just what to do with "Whose Bed Have Your Boots Been Under?" and "Any Man of Mine." Furthermore, it was becoming evident that this alluring newcomer had something every self-respecting moneyman dreams about: crossover potential. She had the power to appeal to people for whom country music was normally a communication from an alternate universe. *The Woman in Me* caught fire, capturing the hearts and imaginations of a broad spectrum of music lovers.

Eight months into 1995, the album went double platinum in both Canada and the United States: it had racked up sales figures of 200,000 copies in Canada and a cool two million in the U.S. It hit number one on the *Billboard* country charts, and on *Billboard*'s general list it climbed to number eight. In both Canada and the U.S., a single from the album, "Any Man of Mine," hit number one, and this made Shania the first Canadian to achieve such a distinction since one of her idols, Anne Murray, pulled it off in 1986. "Whose Bed Have Your Boots Been Under?" *The Woman in Me*'s first single, enjoyed equal success in Canada and made it into the top ten south of the border.

Television and the print media helped to fuel the phenomenon. Shania was suddenly everywhere. Spots on shows like *Regis & Kathy Lee* and *Entertainment Tonight* were matched by feature articles and interviews in such high-profile organs as *Entertainment Weekly*. Newspapers across North America picked up the story and ran with it. Shania (like everybody else involved with *The Woman in Me* — particularly the team at her record company, Mercury Nashville, and her husband-producer, Mutt Lange) was ecstatic. It was all beyond her wildest dreams. And, if the flood had become a trickle at this juncture, Shania — and even the people at Mercury Nashville — would likely have just counted their lucky stars and left it at that. But it didn't end there. *The Woman in Me* spawned several more smash singles, and the album has sold twelve million copies to date ("Brandt").

During the hot, humid summer of 1995, there were no holidays for Shania. It was a breathless season filled with a seemingly endless succession of engagements and appearances, all geared towards maximizing the album's already staggering sales. Shania had so far been granted little time to bask in the glow of her accomplishments. She had trouble absorbing the dimensions of what was happening to her: "I didn't even realize til just recently that I was the first Canadian to top the singles chart since 1986," she told *Network* magazine at the end of August 1995. "I think the speed is what overwhelms me more that anything" ("Shania Sitting").

During one stifling long weekend just days before she would reach another personal milestone — she turned thirty on 28 August 1995 — Shania found herself close to home. On a visit to one of Canada's most famous amusement parks, Canada's Wonderland, located just north of Toronto, she had no time for fun and games. Thousands had turned out to enjoy a day of sunshine and balmy temperatures, and to risk cardiac arrest on gut-scrambling rides with names like *Top Gun*. Shania was mobbed. She had come to cohost a music festival at the park, which was sponsored by a local country-music station. Although not on tour — she wasn't traveling with a backup band — Shania turned out to be the feature attraction.

Over five thousand Wonderland patrons clustered to catch a glimpse of the freshly hatched superstar, and Shania did not disappoint. She had been invited simply to introduce other acts, but the crowd called out for more. They shouted requests. They wanted her to sing. And so she complied. A cappella. Her rousing rendition of "Any Man of Mine," which proved definitively that her vocal skills truly are extraordinary, stopped the show. Shania spent the rest of the afternoon doing what she had been doing since she made the controversial decision not to tour her record in the conventional sense: she met with her fans. She shook hands and posed for photos with anyone who asked. She talked to her fans about her music, her life, their lives — whatever came up. She smiled and laughed and joked with ease, demonstrating her solidarity with her audience, her accessibility, her refusal to indulge in a star trip. Even after the festival had officially ended, Shania was still signing autographs and hanging out.

Still, the next morning she was back at it, stoking the star-maker machinery. In a Toronto studio, beneath a battery of hot lights, Shania posed patiently for a series of photo portraits that were destined for bus shelters and billboards. Another full day of working and waiting, waiting and working. As soon as the last shots had been captured, Shania was whisked to Toronto's Pearson Airport to catch a flight home: as a reward for her hard labor, she was to be permitted a brief spell of rest and relaxation with Mutt. Even her downtime at Pearson was put to good use; she gave several interviews at an airport restaurant while waiting for her plane. She told one interviewer, Nicholas Jennings, that she was drained, but, as he noted, she still looked "casually stunning in a white T-shirt and blue jeans." Shania wisely refused to complain about the wages of her good fortune. A self-pitying celebrity quickly turns off her fans. "It was . . . a lot of work," was all she would say, "but, I've had worse."

At thirty, Shania was already well into the third decade of her career. She'd already experienced a long acquaintance with the rigors of traveling from town to town, gig to gig, in trucks, vans, and buses. The year 1995 may have seen her ascend to the jet-setting ranks, but she still had not forgotten what it was like when she couldn't afford to travel first class. She had definitely "had worse": try planting trees instead of signing autographs under the August sun. The Wonderland appearance was just one of many similar gigs Shania's management and promotional team had set up for her. Photo and video shoots, interviews, award ceremonies, and television appearances filled her days and nights. As Christmas 1995 rolled around, Shania was able to reflect on the year: it had been the most grueling, exhilarating, astonishing twelve-month interlude in her life.

It is important for anyone who wants to understand the phenomenon of Shania Twain's success to understand first something about the conditions, the context, the history that nourished her music. Her art, like everyone else's, is part of a continuum of big names and innovative notions. Shania's mass appeal was made possible by other, earlier trailblazers, and by a general process of upheaval and evolution that was transforming both the country- and pop-music industries.

It had seemed, for a while, that country music was dying a slow and painful death. The genre that had established and maintained its audience through live radio and the roadshow — a genre that truly was of and for the people — appeared poised on the brink of extinction, unable to keep pace with the times. As the music industry at large entered a brave new era, country traditionalists dug in their heels. Instead of adopting new marketing strategies and buying into the technological revolution, they re-pledged their allegiance to the old ways. In time, their stubbornness produced dry rot. Potent symptoms of country's humiliating disease, such as *Hee Haw* (though

Maple Leaf Hotel, local country bar in
Timmins where Shania Twain played

RACHELE LABRECQUE

featuring guitar virtuoso and country giant Roy Clark, this was a relatively banal, family-oriented, *Laugh In*-style country television show of the 1970s) began to crop up. Country and its proud tradition were becoming debased in the popular imagination.

Even such luminaries as Hank Williams, Patsy Cline, and, later, Johnny Cash and Tammy Wynette seemed somehow tarnished. Sixties artists like Roger Miller and Kris Kristofferson, with their maverick talents, did manage to massage some life back into the increasingly moribund Nashville scene, as did members of the 1970s Outlaw Movement such as Waylon Jennings and Willie Nelson, but it still wasn't enough. Country needed a complete transfusion.

It wasn't until the mid-1980s that the life-support efforts of Johnny, Tammy, Waylon, Willie, and company began to show concrete results. In 1985, the work of such previously tradition-bound artists as Ricky Skaggs, George Strait, and Randy Travis began to display a new edge. In 1989, the Nashville scene was finally blown wide open. A whole new breed of country artists emerged, kicking and screaming, with a fresh, exciting sound to offer. Over the course of that year, Clint Black, Garth Brooks, Alan Jackson, and Travis Tritt all released albums that heralded the dawning of an era. The New Country was born.

After years of languishing, country could now serve as a barometer for the health of the entire business in North America. In 1985, the genre accounted for only about six percent of total record sales. By 1989, that figure hovered at the twenty-percent mark. By the mid-1990s, *Network*, a Canadian recording-industry magazine, was estimating that there were upwards of one hundred million country-music fans in Canada and the U.S. Of that number, only twenty-five percent could be considered pre-1985 stalwarts. At least three-quarters of all country fans in the 1990s are post-1980s converts.

Like its American counterpart, the Canadian country-music industry has also grown exponentially since 1985. And also like its American counterpart, it became a dominant force within the nation's cultural borders in the space of just ten years. Shania's 1995 breakthrough was one of the crowning achievements of that decade-long high cycle. Many of Shania's Canadian peers — artists like Michelle Wright, Charlie Major, Prairie Oyster, and Blue Rodeo — also scored hits in 1995. Most sold well over 200,000 copies of their product, but none could touch Shania's sales figures; in Canada, though, where the population stands at only thirty million, a record goes platinum when it reaches sales of 100,000.

Like the new American sound — the country music

that was born in a spirit of revision, innovation, and experimentation at the end of the 1980s — the Canadian New Country has proven to be both audience and artist based: audience based, because it depended on the emergence of a whole new audience drawn from diverse niches of the mainstream record-buying public; artist-based, because without innovators the new sound wouldn't exist. Those innovators blended musical styles with an unprecedented ease. Canadian country of the 1990s, according to music writer Terry Pasieka, has its roots in "five distinct musical genres: 1) western swing, 2) folk, 3) blues, 4) rockabilly, and 5) mid-60s to late-70s classic rock." In Shania's work, it's not difficult to pick out strains of each, but the balance is always maintained: she never relies too heavily on any one.

That country now prevails in Canada is beyond dispute. Witness its power to attract huge audiences. Even though Canadians and Americans weren't treated to a full-blown Shania Twain tour in 1995, the new vitality of country music in Canada can be gauged by the public response to other country acts who did find themselves on the road and crossing borders. In Toronto, on the shore of Lake Ontario, a live-music complex was opened just before Shania appeared at Canada's Wonderland. The Molson Amphitheatre, located on the grounds of Ontario Place, a major tourist attraction, rapidly became one of the nation's premier venues. In the summer of 1995, two shows, one featuring American country superstars Alan Jackson and Faith Hill, and the other Vince Gill and Patty Loveless, drew the second and third largest crowds of the season. Only alternative-rock giants REM managed to pull in more people, and the country showcases outdrew numerous other big-name pop acts, including Canadian rock icon Bryan Adams.

Similarly, New Country's ability to generate advertising revenue for radio and television testifies to the strength of its fan support. And here, of course, Shania played a major role. *The Woman in Me* bought airtime and sold millions of copies. The influx of advertising dollars has meant that more stations can thrive by programming country music. In turn, this has meant more airtime for both American and Canadian country artists. Between the late 1980s and the mid-1990s, the number of country radio stations in Canada grew from between 65 and 75 to between 100 and 110. Toronto's CISS-FM for example, which began broadcasting in 1993, listed three-quarters of a million listeners in its first rating book. Coming out of nowhere, the fledgling station became the second most popular stop on the dial in Canada's music capital. (Subsequently, its audience has tapered a bit, but it still averages 600,000 listeners, making it the third most popular country-music station in North America.) In other, even more country-friendly Canadian cities — Calgary, Alberta, for instance — country radio stations were number one in 1995. In fact, in the mid-1990s you'd be hard pressed to find a single major urban area in Canada where the premier country radio station didn't at least place in the top five in terms of market share.

Of course, Canadian television broadcasters have always reserved a niche for country variety programming. Shania herself performed on several local and national shows while she was a young hopeful from Timmins. Canadian Broadcasting Corporation classics like the *Tommy Hunter Show* metamorphosed in the 1990s into such popular successes as Rita MacNeil's *Rita & Friends*, which helped bring Canadian country to a new generation of viewers. And the presentation ceremony of the annual Canadian Country Music Awards has become an eagerly anticipated television event. By 1995, an estimated 1.5 million viewers were tuning in. That year, the event, hosted by Anne Murray, attracted even more viewers than the Junos — the Canadian music industry's showcase awards ceremony.

So, like their colleagues in radio, Canadian television programmers have also jumped on the country bandwagon. But before seeking out their piece of the pie, Canadian television executives had to make a tough decision: should they pursue country-music audiences, enticing them with a full-time country-music channel, or should they sit tight and avoid the bruising confrontation with their better established and more powerful competitors that such a course of action would entail? Ultimately, the voice of caution was drowned out, and an all-country music video channel, CMT (Country Music Television), was launched when its parent company, Rawlco Communications, was awarded a license in January 1995. The executive decision was the right one. The channel is thriving.

It has also made an enormous difference. Despite the arrival on the national country-music scene of some top-quality homegrown talent, until the mid-1990s the Canadian country market was dominated by American imports. Some commentators, such as Kim Cooke of Warner Music Canada, felt defeated by this state of affairs. "Maybe the Canadian public is simply making its judgment on the Canadian artists it's seeing and hearing," she told *Words & Music* magazine in the fall of 1995, "and not judging those artists favourably" ("Radio Airplay"). Others, however, like Rawlco's Doug Pringle, saw 1995 as a turning point. And they proved to be right. That year, Pringle became the director of programming of both CISS-FM and CMT Canada (which until the autumn of

1996 was called NCN), and this made him one of the most powerful people in the Canadian country world. Like Cooke, Pringle acknowledged that the sales performance of Canadian country artists had been decidedly lackluster, but in his mind the source of the problem was this: the Canadian public had little opportunity to see and hear its own artists.

Until 1995, both of the country video channels available to Canadians were American owned and operated. In fact, all the leading — and highly influential — entertainment beaming into Canadian living rooms originated stateside and featured American performers. From Letterman to Leno, from *Entertainment Tonight* to daytime tabloid TV, Canadians were being fed a steady diet of American pop culture. It should come as no surprise that American artists, not their Canadian brothers and sisters, were the ones making the cash registers ring. It would take radio and television broadcasting initiatives like Pringle's to buck this trend; the enormous growth of Canadian country radio and television programming in the 1990s spearheaded the offensive. Speaking to the same *Words & Music* reporter who had interviewed Cooke, Pringle emphasized the crucial role CMT was fulfilling, tempering his remarks with a note of cautious optimism that Cooke couldn't yet claim to feel: "Now with CMT," he declared, "we're seeing part of the important American machinery available to Canadian artists. So this, along with more focus on 'new country' formats and the emergence of some incredible talent, I think will result in stronger record sales. I see a lot of reason to be encouraged" ("Radio Airplay").

As 1995 wound down, Pringle's predictions were borne out. Canadian country, and Canadian music in general, started to make their presence felt both domestically and internationally. They could no longer be ignored. In 1995,

Nashville, like the rest of the world, was listening to Canadian country artists. And, at last, so was Canada.

Responsibility for this vital consciousness shift didn't rest entirely on Shania's slim shoulders, either. Another young Canadian woman, Alanis Morissette, was doing for pop precisely what Shania was doing for country. Her album *Jagged Little Pill* was released in 1995 by Maverick Warner. It gave birth to the monster singles "You Oughta Know" and the aptly titled "Ironic," and made Alanis, like Shania, another of the fastest-rising stars on the American charts. Critics promptly labeled her "riot girl" and "bitch rocker," and her appeal burgeoned in the gen-X market. Alanis's angst-ridden sound made her as much of a leader in her milieu as Shania was in hers.

The two women are poles apart musically — Shania "exudes soft, sexy romanticism," announced the *Calgary Herald*, while Alanis's "defiant, cutting-edge songs are laced with lyrics designed to shock" (Haysom) — but together they have scaled the world's major music markets. When you throw Céline Dion's 1994 blockbuster *Color of My Love* into the mix — an album that had, by the fall of 1995, itself sold more than ten million copies worldwide — Canada's musical triumph is complete. The time for cautious optimism is over; since the end of 1995, the celebration has been proceeding full tilt. The women from north of the border are now a force to contend with.

Billboard magazine's 1995 year-end double issue was devoted to an assessment of the year's major musical success stories. The cover of this special issue of the industry's leading publication featured six album-cover reproductions. This gallery of winners was *the* place to be, and there were *Jagged Little Pill* and *The Woman in Me*. Shania and Alanis gleaned accolades galore and a truckload of silverware. Both won almost every award offered in their respective musical genres, at home and abroad. By early 1996, appearing on the live broadcasts of award ceremonies had practically become second nature to them.

In January of that year, Shania was honored as one of the brightest international lights in the American entertainment industry at a very unlikely venue. She was asked to sing Canada's national anthem at an NBA all-star game. Her performance was one of a series of impressive signals that country music had accessed the mainstream. Before 1996, it's highly unlikely that NBA brass would have been interested in forging any connection between the urban big business of their basketball association and the musical expressions of America's country heartland. As the new year began, it suddenly seemed like the right thing to do. And the fact that the connection they chose was embodied by Shania Twain, a Canadian, was hard to overlook. In February, the British entertainment industry presented Alanis Morissette with a Brit award for "most promising international newcomer," and Canada's musical impact was compounded.

All of this, however, was just icing on the cake. The serious moment of glory for Canadian musicians in 1995 came when Shania and Alanis led a large contingent of artists from the Great White North in a collective grab for the music industry's supreme honor. Along with internationally renowned Canadian veterans Bryan Adams, Joni Mitchell, and Neil Young, the two women were nominated for Grammies. Shania had received four nominations and Alanis six. They had to know that they were now setting the pace for both their homeland and the industry. To make matters even more interesting, they were competing head to head in the important Best New Artist category (though neither won).

MYRON ZABOL/MERCURY RECORDS

By the time Shania finally had a moment to pause and reflect upon the success of *The Woman in Me*, she had more than twenty-five major industry awards to list on her résumé. One album, one year, had transformed her life. The strength and the artistry of that album, from which she had spun no fewer than eight singles, were eloquent testimony to the fact that she was no overnight sensation, though to some Nashville insiders she must surely have seemed like one. Country acts just didn't explode out of total obscurity to attain superstar status in such a limited amount of time. Shania had blown into town and become one of America's most beloved performers. With their entrenched "If it ain't broken, don't fix it" attitude, country-music executives, to put it mildly, are not known for taking risks. And why should they? There has always been, and there always will be, an abundance of American talent for them to develop and promote. This young Canadian, however, was forcing them to revise their outlook.

She did it first by capturing the hearts and imaginations of country fans (and a host of others) with a sound that was almost completely foreign to Nashville. Departing from the status quo, dispensing with many of Nashville's hallowed rules and traditions, she took a huge risk, but she hit upon a formula that worked. The fans welcomed, accepted, and celebrated this outsider, and now the Nashville establishment had to follow suit. This new attitude was demonstrated for the first time at the 1995 Country Music Association Awards ceremony in Nashville. As the show kicked off, the audience heard the now familiar ba-ba-BAM! ba-ba-BAM! rock-and-roll snare- and bass-drum riff that drives Shania's "Any Man of Mine." At that moment, her place in the industry was assured. Shania Twain, the CMA was saying, was the new standard-bearer. In fact, "Any Man of Mine" not only inaugurated the evening's festivities, but also proved to be the highlight. Shania's sexy, exuberant performance of her hit single soon had everyone talking. And that wasn't surprising. People had been talking about her, by that time, for quite a while. It had been that kind of year.

After Shania had completed her conquest of Nashville, she left the door wide open for other Canadian acts. Most notably, Terri Clark and Paul Brandt have been turning heads in Tennessee. Clark, who was born in Montreal and raised in Moose Jaw, Saskatchewan, has won respect and become one of country's biggest draws by successfully marketing herself as a female "hat act." Brandt, a Calgary native, has employed catchy refrains and rich, booming vocals to propel his singles right up the *Billboard* country charts, and a number of his songs have even reached *Billboard's* coveted number-one position. In the wake of the Shania phenomenon, American country-music labels have begun scouting still more Canadian talent. No longer does a Canadian have to go to Nashville to make it: Nashville movers and shakers are making pilgrimages to Canada.

Shania's meteoric rise wasn't arrested simply because her breakthrough year finally drew to a close; 1995 rolled into 1996 with no sign of a change in momentum. By the time the first anniversary of the release of *The Woman in Me* arrived, sales had topped the five-million mark. The record was still firmly entrenched in *Billboard's* top ten, and new single releases and videos were still being scheduled. Shania's surprise success was yesterday's news. And all of this was happening despite her decision not to tour. In this regard, as well, Shania was forcing industry insiders to rethink the conventional wisdom.

Shania has taken a great deal of flak for that decision. Many industry veterans believed that by refusing to follow the ordained trajectory — record an album, get the thing into the stores, release singles and videos, and then tour like crazy — she was committing career suicide. How could a country performer ever build up a fan base and milk a hit for all its worth without hitting the road? If you can't pull off headliner gigs, then at least open for a bigger act. Some actually seemed to resent Shania for not playing the game. Furthermore, it was almost as though, with her sexy videos and big studio sound loaded with crossover potential, she was diluting the purity of the music they loved. So the rumor mill was fired up to produce a little revenge. It worked like this: the word got around that Shania wasn't touring because Shania couldn't sing.

While it would be foolish to minimize the importance of production values to the success of *The Woman in Me* — producer Mutt Lange's skill and vision have left their prominent imprint on every track — it would also be patently false to say that Shania's voice was processed and altered to create a saleable record. Shania has not hesitated to elaborate the real reasons behind her rejection of the touring option. To one interviewer she remarked: "I had toured basically as a no one for many years. Right from childhood, driving across the country singing in clubs to people who didn't know who the heck I was or what the songs were all about. I did that up to this album. When [*The Woman in Me*] came out, I had such confidence in it I thought it deserved its chance to prove itself musically before I tried to sell it with a concert" (Cohen). Elsewhere, she revealed a little more: "What I have done with this album," she contended, "is take a break and say, 'Listen, I want to tour with a real roster of songs behind me that are going to support the show as opposed to the show supporting the songs'" (Tarradell).

Ultimately, Shania's decision had been based on two realizations she came to after a lot of soul-searching. The first was that she truly did not feel, despite the success of so many of the cuts from *The Woman in Me*, that she had enough material to give her fans the kind of show they deserved. "I don't want to get out there and give everything at once, just to get all the money I can," she insisted ("No Live Shows"). She wanted "to allow some time for these songs to prove themselves," because "the music has to lead the way." When she felt her act was ready, when, simply, she had "enough songs to plan a good hour or hour-and-a-half show of songs that people are familiar with," she would tour (Tarradell). It was a promise.

The second realization was equally important to Shania. She had to avoid both overexposure and burnout. "I like to think I'm playing it smart," she commented: "I want my career to last." If she toured solely on the strength of her *Woman in Me* hits, then "everybody would be fed up of seeing me on TV, hearing me on radio and seeing me twice in concert in the same year" ("No Live Shows"). To ensure that her appeal endured, Shania was convinced, she had to do things differently. And that included completely rethinking how and why she would tour. "We just want to put together the best live show we can and tour with that rather than go out and spend most of the year on the road, like everybody else. I guess that's the way country acts do it, but that's not how rock acts do it. Country could learn a lot more from rock" (Richmond). This attitude, to her Nashville critics, was tantamount to blasphemy.

For many, country is country precisely because it has resisted the temptation to market itself like rock. One of the basic tenets of country has always been to maintain a low profile, to keep things on a no-frills, grassroots level.

Platinum party with Mercury staff
BETH GWINN

Rock's promotional strategies are alien to this philosophy. But, to Shania's thinking, the sky's the limit. There is no reason country can't become an even bigger phenomenon than it already is. Country's reputation for being antipop has to be overcome; crossing over must be accepted as a vital part of the genre's evolution. Muses Shania: "I entertain the thought that maybe a Mariah Carey fan has a Shania Twain album. I wonder who those fans are, who else is in their record collections" (Powell). Those are the kind of fans, she believes, that country artists have to reach.

In her bid to position her own disc within those broad-based collections, Shania had her work cut out for her. She would have to be as good as the best contemporary pop-rock had to offer. She would not only have to contend with country heavyweights, but she would also be obliged to compete for the public's attention with MTV megastars, supermodels, and movie icons. Everything she did would have to make an impact. With her management team, she scrutinized every detail of the Shania Twain marketing strategy; absolutely nothing was left to chance. And no sacrifice, it seems, was too great. Instead of sitting back on the tour bus, like other country artists, as it trekked from Oklahoma City to the Ozarks, Shania subjected herself to a five-hour fitting for a video shoot. Was pouring such copious amounts of energy and money into an outfit destined to be worn for just three and a half minutes of screen time a frivolous waste? Not to Shania. Allowing herself to be sewn into the bell-bottomed pants that lent such panache to the "Outta Here" video was a sound business decision — no more and no less. All such activity, she felt, was a necessary part of being an entertainer in the 1990s.

Shania's conviction that the time had come for country performers to accept certain realities of the entertainment business never wavered. "Listen," she told the *Village Voice*, "the audience had sophisticated ears — and eyes. The audience that watches any kind of television and listens to any kind of audio gets the top quality just through ads. Hey, they have to be able to go from a Coke ad or a Janet Jackson record to my record and not notice a difference in quality. There's no reason that we shouldn't be at that level. That's absolutely been my goal from the beginning" (Leamer). On another occasion, she picked up the gauntlet again: "Our job in country music right now as artists has to be to keep those listeners that would just as soon turn over to a light rock or adult contemporary station. We have to give those people what they want to hear in order to keep them there. They love to hear the rock influence, the blues influence, all the influences that are also considered very American" (Leamer).

Gradually, some of the players began to listen. The head

of the Country Music Association, Ed Benson, conceded that Shania's marketing strategies could influence the way country musicians would do business in the future. "Whatever happened to four guys in a van," he joked ruefully. "The way it's been for a long, long time is you have a hit, immediately you buy a bus and hire a band and tour all year round to support the payroll you've taken on" (Patterson, "Shania Twain"). That's the way Patsy and Loretta did it. And it's what the Judds and Reba McEntire have done. Shania, however, sold her album by putting the electronic media to work for her.

Her sexy videos got fans hooked on her songs, and then she focused her energies on maintaining a high public profile and making her next release even more spectacular than its predecessor. The combination of a sultry but down-home image, catchy, rhythmic songs, provocative but fun lyrics, and just a hint of mystery paid off in spades. The videos generated enough attention to keep *The Woman in Me* in the public eye and sales strong.

So strong, in fact, that a number of other Nashville heavy hitters were inspired to reformulate their approaches. Garth Brooks, for one, spent most of 1995 lying low, putting the finishing touches on his album *Fresh Horses* and conserving his energies for its Christmas release. Of the few shows Brooks gave that year, most took place in Europe, where he and his record company hoped to cultivate a new fan base. Clint Black, as well, decided to put his bus in the garage. Late in 1995, he announced that he was going to take at least a year off. He thought he might venture overseas to do a few gigs, but he needed to recover from his stressful — yet rewarding — tour of America.

By early 1996, Shania had clearly become expert at creating and sustaining her own professional image. She had mastered the art of the public appearance. "Never before," Leamer notes, "had there been a performer in country who spent her days in endless self-promotion. There were pop stars such as Barbra Streisand and Mariah Carey who never or rarely toured, but they did not spend their days as Shania did." Shania spent many of her days connecting with her fans. In country music, stars and fans have traditionally enjoyed closer relations than they have in other sectors of the business. The meet-and-greet is a well-established activity. Shania, like most other country performers, has long believed that these events, epitomized by Nashville's annual Fan Fair, are the lifeblood of the country-music industry. Within a year of *The Woman in Me*'s release, she could have conducted seminars in the touring fan fair. In a series of daily appearances described by one critic as the "marvel of marketing genius known as Fan Appreciation Day," Shania went to meet the people in their own backyards (Schoemer).

Throughout 1996, she crisscrossed North America, shaking hands, signing autographs, and thanking her fans for rocketing her into the superstar stratosphere. She consistently presented them with that finely crafted superstar image they knew from her videos, and they were not disappointed: Shania in the flesh matched the video Shania perfectly. By the time her tour hit the Mall of America in Minneapolis, Americans had begun to think of Shania, a Canadian, as their new, unofficial Miss America. At least ten thousand people crammed themselves into the state-of-the-art shopping plaza, and each individual in this sea of humanity was there for the same reason: to get close to Shania.

Wherever she went that year, the scene kept replaying itself. The Fan Appreciation Days, especially, felt like huge stadium shows. Of course, there was no live stage show, but for most of those fans standing in line to meet their idol, the trade-off was well worth it. Instead of existing for them as a tiny speck on a distant stage for an hour or ninety minutes, Shania was right there, among them, talking, smiling, hugging, and laughing, for about four hours.

This was the drill: after the crowds had gathered, drawn by huge, colorful banners and posters and a wall of giant television monitors playing Shania's videos in a continuous loop, a record-company rep would pump up the crowd and introduce the star. At the Mall of America, things got quite feverish. The event got under way with the reading of a declaration from the governor of Minnesota proclaiming the day to be Shania Twain Day. Shania then took the stage to thunderous applause. Stepping up to the podium, her electronic image singing, dancing, and cavorting behind her, she appeared to have walked right out of her own video. There she was, the diminutive real thing, but still somehow larger than life. That day, her hair was pulled into a majestically sculpted ponytail. She wore a cropped red turtleneck that revealed an enticing sliver of her toned abdomen (that glimpse of navel had by now become a Shania Twain signature). Her curvy hips were hugged by a pair of black stretch pants. She looked fantastic.

After taking the Mall of America (and after that, what's left of Middle America to conquer?), Shania admitted that she was fully aware of what she was doing — presenting herself as people had come to expect her to be, playing a part, donning an appropriate costume. "Myself personally," she remarked, "I'm very conservative. On my personal time I dress very conservatively, and I'm very old-fashioned. But I believe in entertainment. I think it's a very cool thing. It's almost like I get to step outside of myself and just kind of be this person. I think that's my job: to be this person in the videos that's just free and getting into the music and having fun" (Schoemer). And it's a job she can perform like no one else.

When the introductions have been made, when Shania has extended her thank-yous (and you actually get the sense that her true feelings of gratitude haven't worn off), when the visual punch of her arrival on the video-illuminated scene has been effectively delivered, then the typical Fan Appreciation Day is in full stride. For four hours, sometimes more, Shania strives to make everybody happy, smiling all the while, and signing literally thousands of autographs. Writer's cramp alone could defeat someone of a weaker constitution. She signs everything in sight. A seemingly endless succession of supporters thrust CDs and posters and cassettes at her, each hoping for a few seconds of one-on-one. She scrawls her name on T-shirts, ballcaps, boxer shorts, and they are transformed into talismans. Anyone who asks is allowed to set up his or her very own photo op; disposable Kodaks crop up everywhere. Even young men bold enough to ask for an innocent kiss are accommodated: Fan Appreciation Day is just that kind of event; Shania is reluctant to say no.

As we head into the next millennium, it is apparent that the nature of celebrity has undergone a sea change. The average superstar has become increasingly aloof and reclusive — some are now downright aggressive in their efforts to maintain the impenetrable barrier they have erected between themselves and their fans. Shania has refused to follow suit. She won't insulate herself with an impressive contingent of burly security guys with wireless lapel mikes and earpieces. This is not to say that Shania is unrealistic. She does, of course, have a security team. It's just that her protectors are more discreet than most;

they have been made to understand that their charge is doing what she has to do, that she's mingling with the crowd because that's where she wants to be.

At each of her meet-and-greets, Shania moves from caring, "just plain folks" mode to superstar mode and back again in the blink of an eye. She makes the transition look seamless. Winding up a brief personal chat with an ardent admirer, she'll leap onto a stack of video monitors and start dancing and lip-synching to one of her hits. The crowd always goes wild. On another occasion, she may allow herself to be coaxed into an "impromptu" performance — her fans are always asking, especially, for "Any Man of Mine" — and she'll undertake it either unaccompanied or backed by a few local musicians she's rounded up. Such minispectacles quickly dispel any lingering doubts about the quality and strength of her voice or her ability to turn in a rock-solid live performance. These versions of her songs may be stripped down, but they are clean — and volatile.

If, by 1996 in the U.S.A., Shania had become Miss Middle America — or Our Lady of the Mall — then in Canada she was both the Queen of the Fairground and one of the nation's most beloved daughters. In fact, almost a year to the day after her Wonderland appearance, she returned home to bestow on Toronto its very own Fan Appreciation Day. It was August, less than two weeks before her thirty-first birthday, and once more Shania found herself entering a teeming amusement park, though this one was set in the heart of Toronto on the grounds of the Canadian National Exhibition. The "CNE" refers to both a sprawling lakeside complex of walkways and structures designed to accommodate various forms of entertainment and industry and a month-long, late-summer festival that began as an agricultural fair in the 1840s. This unique amalgamation of special-interest exhibits — from animal shows, to a celebration of culinary treats from around the world, to live-entertainment showcases and cultural displays — and carnival midway has always been, for both locals and tourists, one of the highlights of a Toronto summer. Every day from dawn until late at night, the CNE pulsates with activity. For decades, the CNE bandshell and the special stage set up in Exhibition Stadium have featured the biggest names in the entertainment industry. It's *the* place to be.

Rumors that Shania was bringing her roadshow to the CNE made their way into the Toronto papers months before the fair was officially opened. By the time August rolled around, Shania's appearance, scheduled for the seventeenth of the month, had become one of the most anticipated events of the summer. For Toronto, it was a brand new concept. Unlike American country-music fans, most Canadian aficionados had never experienced a fan fair and had no idea what to expect. Still, their excitement mounted steadily.

Some fervent supporters, like sixteen-year-old Dylan Mitobe, found it very hard to wait. Mitobe was determined to be the first in line for Shania's autograph. Accompanied by a group of friends, he secured that prized position for himself, but in order to do so he'd had to arrive on the site many hours before his idol was scheduled to appear. Thousands of others soon joined Mitobe and his cohorts. For all concerned, the wait was a negligible price to pay. Shania was three minutes late. The throng's tiny reserve of patience was quickly exhausted. Hundreds began to yell "We Want Shania!" Of course, Shania soon materialized, glowing, joyful, ready to give herself to the clamoring masses. The roar of the crowd was deafening. The summer sun blazed relentlessly.

The crush of bodies was, in places, nearly overwhelming. Yet no one went home feeling let down.

Of all Shania's Fan Appreciation Day appearances, this was perhaps the most satisfying. As a child, she had seen Toronto as a source of the musical education she'd yearned for. As a young adult, she'd lived in the city for a short while — another aspiring performer among so many others, all pursuing dreams of stardom. So, on this hot August day, she looked right at home. Even more relaxed than usual. In her element. It was also apparent that since the Canada's Wonderland love-in of the previous August a fundamental change had taken effect. Everything was so much more intense now, so much more cathartic. A year earlier, everyone had sensed that Shania was on the verge of something great; now she enjoyed a level of fame and adoration that no one would have thought possible. Toronto's Fan Appreciation Day, an event that Shania had planned as a means of thanking her Canadian fans for helping to make her music so popular, really turned out to be Canada's way of acknowledging what Shania meant to Canadians, of welcoming her home. But her biggest homecoming, the one that was layered with the most significance, had already occurred. Just days earlier, 15 August 1996, Timmins had celebrated Shania Twain Day.

By midsummer, the Native-heritage controversy that had dogged Shania throughout the spring had all but blown over. Though some nagging doubts about what had motivated her to alter her history persisted, most reporters and fans considered the issue closed. The fact that the scandal had originated in her hometown was no doubt disturbing for Shania; many in her position would have allowed themselves to become embittered; the whole mess reeked of jealousy and betrayal. Shania, however, finally chose to take a philosophical approach to it all — at least publicly. Scandal, she reasoned, just seemed to come with the territory. A celebrity had to take these things in stride.

So, on returning home to Timmins with such fanfare, Shania was assailed with mixed emotions. A load of memories descended and collided with a new set of realities. It was Eileen Twain who left this town with Nashville firmly in her sights — a fairly inconspicuous local girl, the one with the beautiful voice and the lofty goals. But by 15 August 1996, she had become Shania — the most famous citizen Timmins was ever likely to produce, the town's prized export, its pride and joy. Timmins wanted to claim a little of Shania's stardom.

Timmins is a bustling regional hub that's home to more than forty thousand people. Its economy depends mainly on the mining industry; the Kidd Creek mine, which is arguably the largest and most important producer of zinc and silver in the world, is located there. Like any American town of the same size, it has all the amenities. Still, outsiders don't know much about the place, and the locals don't seem to mind in the least. "Let them be surprised when they get here," is their attitude. These are not the kind of people who like to blow their own horn. For the most part, Timmins is a hard-working, close-knit, blue-collar type of town where people put stock in the simpler things of life. Here, community matters. Local concerns are dealt with locally.

In the past, the primary objects of the town's civic pride were young men. Most of its favorite sons are hockey stars lauded for their toughness, for their ability to play the game the way it was meant to be played. The character of these local heroes reflects the character of their hometown: no-nonsense, loyal, conservative, traditional. Their successes have brought honor to their community, and

Timmins has shown its gratitude. The fame that these men achieved, however, was circumscribed. The national spotlight rested on them for awhile, but their following consisted almost entirely of Canadian hockey fans. Their renown crossed few borders. It took a daughter of Timmins, Shania Twain, to break through. Her international superstar status astounded her fellow citizens; they still hadn't recovered by 15 August 1996, and perhaps never would. Shania had altered their sense of themselves in the global village. A young Timmins megafan named Chris Bourgeouis put it this way: "This is probably how people in Liverpool felt when the Beatles became famous" (Dunphy). Shania may not have been "bigger than Jesus," but her celebrity was vast.

Timmins prepared for her return as though for a coronation. The town was pumped. Planning for Shania Twain Day had been initiated early, and by the morning of 15 August the excitement was peaking. Outside Timmins City Hall, the crowds thickened. Banners flew, people lined the streets, jostling for position. A cold rain pelted down — at times in torrents — but the general mood seemed squelch-proof. It looked like this was to be the kind of homecoming you always thought only existed in novels and movies.

A public-address system blared Shania's hits, and the assembled, now several thousand strong, clapped and sang along. They joyfully completed the chorus of "Any Man of Mine" in perfect unison. When a police cruiser followed by a silver stretch limo finally pulled up in front of City Hall, thunderous applause broke out. The object of all this adulation slid out from the vehicle's cushy interior, and the decibel level shot even higher. Standing in the rain, a small security and administrative entourage and her ever-loyal Tim in tow, Shania smiled a huge, dazzling, and utterly genuine smile. She had arrived in town a couple of days earlier to spend some time with her family, but for her legion of local fans the reunion began at that moment.

Dressed in her trademark hip-hugging black pants, a tight-fitting, high-necked, yellow-and-blue sweater, and a stylish white jacket, Shania looked every inch the star, but she was visibly moved by the tremendous outpouring of emotion that greeted her. Her eyes darted as she scanned the crowd, and she breathed in deep draughts of the Timmins air. Intermittent cries of "Shania!" she rewarded with a wave of her hand and even more smiles.

After being officially welcomed by Timmins mayor Vic Power — whom Shania had known as the guidance-department head while she was a student at Timmins High and Vocational School — as well as a number of city councillors, Shania took the opportunity, once again, to turn her day into something more all-embracing. Addressing the crowd, she made it clear that she viewed the event as more than a moment of personal honor; it was also a way for her to thank Timmins and to celebrate her roots. Not even the weather could spoil the moment. "This is definitely going to be a bad hair day for the whole city of Timmins," she cracked, making reference to the lyrics of "Any Man of Mine." "We're tough, we're not made of sugar. . . . We're Northerners. . . . We can deal with the weather!" (Kovach). She'd gauged the day, the mood, the crowd perfectly; her words were met with a roar of approval.

"I left Timmins in pursuit of a worldwide career," she went on to tell her audience. "I feel like the same person as when I left town but now I'm treated like a queen. . . . This is overwhelming!" (Hickey). As she said this her voice wavered; the tide of hometown support had touched her more profoundly than anything else had in the past year.

As the day progressed, Timmins continued to broadcast its love and approval loud and clear, but even the province of Ontario and the rest of Canada managed to get in on the action. The province's premier, Mike Harris, sent his congratulations, and added, with reference to the huge success of "(If You're Not in It for Love) I'm Outta Here," that even if she was "outta here" she'd always be remembered as a Canadian. And although many of the people who had turned out to greet her merely had to open their front doors and walk out into the street, others had traveled great distances to join the celebration. One fifteen year old from British Columbia, Lori Olson, held a sign that read: "I travelled over 2,500 miles to meet Shania" (Kovach). Standing in the rain, clutching a freshly signed Shania Twain autograph, she gushed: "This is really great for me. It made my trip worth it." When Lori then remarked, "I don't really listen to country that much, only to Shania Twain," she put a human face on the vast new market segment that had made *The Woman in Me* a worldwide, red-hot commodity and had prompted similar adulation fests (Liersch and Reyes).

At one point, Shania bolted away from the side of her increasingly exasperated bodyguard and plunged into the crowd to embrace an old friend. The woman, a pal from Shania's high school days, produced a copy of their grad yearbook and showed Shania what she had written there so many years before. "This signature could be worth millions someday," young Eileen had scrawled. Both the moment and the memento were priceless. The look on Shania's face said it all, but she commented, laughing, "Isn't it amazing that I wrote that? Why would I have written that?" ("Gold Country"). The answer is obvious:

she wrote those words because even as a teenager her belief in herself was fierce, and she knew she would be prepared to do almost anything to realize her aspirations.

Vic Power kept the honors coming. After all, Shania was every mayor's dream come true. As Power had told a reporter earlier that year, "Shania has not forgotten her roots. Every single interview she mentions Timmins" (Dunphy). So she was given the key to the city, the first Timmins had ever awarded. A special guitar-shaped garden was planted in a Timmins park to commemorate her achievement. Finally, the ultimate tribute was bestowed upon her: to acknowledge her civic contribution — the link she had forged between her hometown and Nashville, between Timmins and the world — a section of highway, Algonquin Boulevard, was renamed Shania Twain Way. A billboard towering over that stretch of asphalt features Shania as she appears on the cover of *The Woman in Me*; today, the first face you are likely to see upon entering Timmins is Shania's. Pressing her hands into cement at the dedication ceremony, she seemed overawed at the thought of literally becoming a part of the Timmins infrastructure. "You don't get a highway dedicated to you every day," she said.

As this extraordinary day wore on, it became more apparent that Shania was not simply there to absorb whatever accolades the town would throw at her: she was on a pilgrimage of sorts; she was actively reconnecting with her past, with the place that had helped shape who she was. Accordingly, she spent some time honoring her Native heritage — personal, familial, and communal. Planting a tree in memory of her late grandfather, she paid homage both to the Twain family and her Native ancestry. The sapling was a living reminder of the time she had toiled in the Twain reforestation business, of her family's day-to-day struggle to survive. "This is a symbol of replacing some of what we take from nature," Shania explained as she settled the tree's roots into the earth (Liersch and Reyes).

Before the tree-planting ceremony, at a public luncheon, the Native community of Timmins demonstrated that it understood Shania and stood solidly behind her. The Mattagami First Nation surprised her with a declaration of support for her claim to a Native identity, and by virtue of this action eased the residual pain of the heritage scandal that had marred Shania's spring. Being honored publicly by her people made the day even sweeter and more satisfying. If she had made this journey home in part to rediscover the place where she truly belonged, wherever she might wander, she had succeeded. Reassured that she had roots that would withstand any storm, Shania could take on the world with confidence.

The time had come to cap the festivities. A one-hundred-dollar-a-plate gala benefit dinner was held that night with Shania as guest of honor. Again, she was treated like royalty. It was a magical, black-tie event; on such an occasion, those surreptitiously consumed mustard sandwiches of her childhood must have seemed to Shania like some dim relic from another life. In a sheer, black evening gown, Shania glowed like Cinderella at the ball. The evening had a pull-out-the-stops Hollywood awards-ceremony feel. Two muscular young men, their naked upper bodies painted gold, served as Shania's escorts. The red carpet was literally rolled out.

The highlight of the occasion was a unique conception. Struck by the way Shania's songs had bridged the gap between individual taste and both popular and more esoteric musical genres, the conductor of the Timmins Symphony Orchestra, Geoff Lee, had composed a waltz to celebrate and reflect her accomplishment. As the orchestra performed the piece, "high" and "low" cultures embraced. When the last notes of "Twain's Waltz" had faded, it was clear that Shania was deeply moved. This delicate, classical composition was a ringing endorsement of her musical skill and importance, and, as such, it was very precious. "Twain's Waltz," compounded by all the other honors, was also a vindication of all the difficult choices Shania had been forced to make.

As far as most Timmins residents knew, Shania's August 1996 visit was her first since the fall of 1993, when she had performed back-to-back concerts at a local French-language high school. Then, the town's welcome had been warm, but it paled in comparison to this. The 1993 shows had been arranged as a means of showcasing her debut album, *Shania Twain*, and only the first had sold out. By 1996, it seemed as though Shania could fill the same venue perpetually.

She had, however, returned to Timmins in the interim, but not in a public capacity. Early in 1995, she had slipped back into town without fanfare. Just as her new album poised for take-off, she had learned that her grandfather Twain was terminally ill. Needing to be with family, she rushed home; needing to protect her own privacy and that of the Twain clan, she kept a low profile. Shania stayed by her grandfather's hospital bedside, maintaining a vigil through the night. He died the next day. After the funeral, Shania left Timmins as inconspicuously as she had come. Returning to the United States, she mourned the loss of this beloved elder and felt her resolve to succeed, and thereby bring honor to his memory, deepen.

★ ★ ★

Shania Twain Day in Timmins; Shania Twain Way; "Twain's
Waltz"; Shania's rush to her grandfather's bedside, and
the tree that in his memory spreads its roots, year by
year, deeper into Timmins soil: all these moments and
testimonials bear out one simple truth. Shania never
actually left Timmins. She'll always carry a piece of it with
her, wherever she goes.

Of course, as a young adult, she just had to get out of
town. Most of her cohorts suffered the same itch. Teens
in small cities and towns across North America always
have and still do. Joelle Kovach, Timmins native and
journalism student, describes its local manifestations: "On
a typical evening, the local Tim Horton's donut shop is
crowded with bored teenagers making plans to move
to bustling cities as soon as they finish high school." While
others just dreamed of escape and sketched their itiner-
aries over coffee, Shania labored to make it happen. She
had crushes and boyfriends but somehow summoned up
the self-restraint to ensure that they didn't complicate her
life or infringe on her long-term goals. Anyway, her heart
always seemed to lead her back to music; this is something
that anyone who wanted to figure in Eileen Twain's world
had to accept.

Other teenage preoccupations, too, were generally sacrificed for the good of her career. Her contemporaries may
have been fully engaged in rebelling against all forms of
authority, but Shania was spread far too thin to join them.
When she wasn't helping around the house, studying, or
holding down an after-school job, she was practicing or
performing her music. "In high school I played in bands
every weekend," Shania explains. "I never drank because
it just wasn't something you did when you were working.
I missed my high school graduation ceremony because I
had to go on the road with my band" (Hager).

Dave Hartt played keyboards with that band. He first heard Shania during one of the regular jam sessions he did with a group of Timmins-based musicians. Taking a break, he ordered pizza and turned on the television. There she was, performing on a local telethon. "Everybody in the room just stopped," he says, "we saw a very pretty girl but that voice! We had to get her to sing with us" (Dunphy). Eventually, she did. The group went by the name The Longshot, and Shania rapidly became an irreplaceable member. Along with Hartt, she led the band towards its goal to succeed not as a country act but as a rock-and-roll band. At first, they presented themselves as a contemporary cover combo, and those who saw them readily acknowledge that they were good — very good. Hartt himself claims that the band was one of the premier rock acts in Timmins at the time, and certainly the best he'd ever belonged to. For their first-ever live gig, they managed to pack the bar by 10 P.M. Even then, performing out of her genre, Shania was spectacular. PJ's Club, one of the band's regular Timmins venues, was wise to have gambled on The Longshot.

Hartt no longer plays with a band, but he's kept in touch with the music biz by managing a record store. Occasionally, people will still ask him what ever happened to the various members of The Longshot. He explains: "a couple of them are involved in a family business, another's in computers, and one guy has even become a business executive." When they ask about the girl singer, however, he merely points to a large autographed poster of Shania on the record-store wall and says, "You mean her?" (Dunphy).

The Longshot disbanded because, Hartt confides, he and Shania "were the two strongest egos," and they eventually "butted heads." Still, despite their differences, which were primarily musical ones, Shania, Hartt, and crew had this in common: "We were all musically driven," Hartt recalls — "single minded." When Shania wasn't performing, she put in time hanging with the rest of the guys; they would practice and talk about music all night long. The Longshot created some good, solid music and shared a few brief highs. And though they eventually had to realize that they couldn't go on together, Hartt is not afraid to admit the obvious: "Ultimately," he says, "she was right" (Dunphy).

Her talent, her work ethic, and her belief in herself, then, are what finally led Shania out of Timmins, follow-ing the road to country-music stardom. Returning home so many years later for Shania Twain Day, she was able to gauge how far she'd really come. Singing, as a three year old, perched on a coffeeshop counter; performing a few years later for after-hours tavern patrons; making television appearances; undertaking music lessons as an adolescent; putting in long hours composing songs in the high school music room; practicing tirelessly, as a teen, with The Longshot: all that focus, positive thinking, and sheer hard work had culminated in a series of wonderful rewards.

On 15 August 1996, Timmins elected to celebrate that very fact. This day was about acknowledging Shania's indefatigable spirit. Yet despite all the excitement and adulation, the festivities were subtly underscored by a current of sadness. It was inevitable that this homecoming would evoke in Shania a profound sense of loss, a keen awareness of an empty space that could never be filled.

Philosophically and spiritually, Shania had come to terms with the 1987 death of her parents years before. It had been an enormous struggle. There was so much she longed to share with them. "The only thing that would make all of this sweeter is if mom and dad were still by my side," she said in the spring of 1993, commenting on the moderate success of her debut album. "But I know they're watching from up there, so I guess they know all about it" (Delaney, "What Made Her"). More than three years later, on Shania Twain Day, these sentiments seemed all the more poignant. The legions of adoring fans, the reunions with old friends, the banquets, the honors — all of this was uplifting for Shania. But the most significant moments of that unforgettable 1996 home-coming occurred when she visited the cemetery where Sharon and Jerry are buried.

5

GOD BLESS THE CHILD

By the late fall of 1987, Shania had already made some life-altering decisions. She'd been out of high school for several years and was beginning to come into her own as a mature and self-reliant young woman. Even though she was still only twenty-two, she had already enjoyed some professional success, as a child country-music performer. Before a succession of live audiences, she'd sung many of her own compositions and covered a respectable range of country classics, she'd opened shows for relatively big-name acts, and she'd been featured on some of Canada's most important country-music television programs.

In northern Ontario, at least, she had developed a name as a promising young vocalist, and word was slowly beginning to spread across the country. Shortly after graduating from high school, she had hooked up with Cree singer-songwriter Lawrence Martin, now a successful Canadian recording artist in his own right. Together they played gigs in Ontario, and even found themselves filling venues as far away as British Columbia. Shania had put in some quality time fronting The Longshot, and with that rock act had played the club circuit and garnered a reputation for being able to sing anything — and sing it well.

By the mid-1980s, Shania was in hot pursuit of her musical dream and gaining a little ground. In December of 1984, her picture was featured for the first time in a national publication — *Country Music News*. It was a studio portrait of a casually beautiful, relaxed, and teenaged Shania, and it accompanied an article about popular Toronto DJ and record producer Stan Campbell's plans for 1985. Campbell's most serious plan involved Shania (then still Eileen), whom he was "especially excited" to work with. "[T]here was no doubt in [Campbell's] mind that Eileen will achieve her goal to become a world-class performer" the *News* reported, and went on to inform its readers that "Eileen possesses a powerful voice with an impressive range." Furthermore, "she has the necessary drive, ambition, and positive attitude that are needed to achieve her goals" ("Producer").

Shania's association with Campbell led to her first significant recording experience and gave her an initial taste of what it would be like to take Nashville. In 1985, Campbell brought an eager young Eileen Twain into the recording studio and produced a lovely duet. Her performing partner was DJ and country singer Tim Denis, and the song was Denis's "Heavy on the Sunshine." The track was released later that year on Denis's self-titled debut album. This vocal credit, and the distinction of having worked with Campbell, were Shania's ticket to reenter the studio, this time with producer Tony Migliore.

The power of Shania's voice impressed Migliore, and he decided to use her as a backup vocalist for a project he was working on with the Canadian artist Kelita. That project was Kelita's album *Too Hot to Handle*, and it was recorded on the RCA label. When the disc made it into

"Eileen" Twain with the cast of "Viva Ve

Macy's Thanksgiving Day Parade, 1995

Shania and Pat Boone,
24th American Music
Awards, Los Angeles, 199

cademy of Country Music Award for Album of the Year, April 1996

hania and Alvin Chea

Shania and Faith Hill

Shania and Céline Di[on]
1996 World Music Aw[ards]

record-store racks later that year, Shania could be heard on the title cut. It was her first contribution to a major-label release, and it was a hit.

Yet despite these feathers in her cap, in some respects Shania was floundering. Her problem was threefold: she was still too young, some industry insiders believed, to be taken seriously; she hadn't been able to make a definitive choice about what musical direction to take, and was still squandering her energies by vacillating between the country she loved and the rock that packed the most lucrative and exciting Canadian venues; finally, and perhaps most importantly, she was struggling to break free of the small-town mind-set. But, as far as Shania was concerned, there was no time to sit around griping about growing pains or indulging in artistic angst.

By 1987, The Longshot had disbanded for the same reasons that most promising young acts fail: artistic differences compounded by lethargy. At this juncture, Shania could have decided to go for a career in pop with any number of other bands. Throughout the late 1980s, she actually did give it a shot, working gigs with several acts, but she quickly discovered that the highs and lows were just the same, and the odds were just as long. It was all a lot of fun; the thrill of performing for revved-up audiences consisting primarily of people her own age was undeniable.

At the end of the day, though, she sensed she was treading water. No matter how exhilarating a particular gig was, she always seemed to be walking home, in her own words, "alone at 3 A.M. with a rock in my pocket" (Johnson). Timmins and the surrounding area now seemed to have so little to offer her. When she wasn't on the road with a touring act, she had the family reforestation business to fall back on, but it was far from enough. Gaining access to fresh opportunities was all she could think about. So she did the obvious thing. She moved to Toronto. One big step out.

Timmins generally and the Twain homestead in particular were safe, familiar enclaves. Leaving them was an emotional wrench. Having skipped the teenage-rebellion phase, Shania was still extraordinarily close to her family, and letting go of her people was on one level like severing a lifeline. Furthermore, her heart and soul belonged to the northern bush that rings Timmins. Still, she knew that if she was ever going to make it she'd have to head south, and the sooner the better; so, by the fall of 1987, she was living on her own, for the first time, in a city where she was just one face among millions.

Toronto was then — as it is now — the nation's musical nerve center. Of course, an array of bands and individual musicians thrive in towns and urban centers from Vancouver on the Pacific to Halifax on the Atlantic, and they will continue to do so — almost every community can support some local talent. But in the Canadian music biz, the money, contacts, and power are concentrated in the heart of downtown Toronto.

It didn't take Shania long to set up a new life for herself in Toronto. She never lost sight of what she was there for, and because she was by nature focused and practical she wasted no time. By night, she put everything into her music, rehearsing religiously and performing whenever she could. By day, she studied and worked as a secretary at a computer school. The job paid the rent on the apartment she'd found and furnished her with the other essentials of life. But Toronto was such a big, fast-paced, and alienating city that at times an oppressive sense of isolation and alienation bore down on Shania.

As an itinerant performer, she had become accustomed

to the loneliness of the road — it had bolstered her already
remarkable self-reliance — but for the first time in her
life she was without her family entirely. For the first time
in her life, the roof over her head was her own, and the
only responsibilities she had were to herself. The freedom
was both stimulating and depressing. She missed having
her little brothers and her younger sister around. They
were her kindred spirits. She still worried about them;
after all, she had been helping to raise them for a long
time, and still fervently wanted to share in their lives. She
missed Sharon and Jerry, too. Acutely. Now, more than
ever, she needed their active support and unconditional
love. Shania called home regularly. The long-distance
charges were steep, but the calls were worth every penny.
This fragile, intermittent connection to Timmins kept
her grounded, kept her in touch with Sharon and Jerry,
her major source of advice and inspiration.

★ ★ ★

On 1 November 1987, everything changed. The world
was turned upside down. Shania's Toronto sojourn ended
abruptly, tragically, when she picked up the telephone
and heard the voice of her older sister, Jill. Her tone
was hushed, devastated. Shania knew almost immediately
that something was terribly wrong. Then Jill told her that
Sharon and Jerry were dead. "All they heard was a horn,"
Shania says, "and that was it" (Jennings). They were killed
instantly when the Chevy Suburban they were driving
collided head-on with a fully loaded logging truck on a
highway near Wawa, Ontario. Shania's carefully erected
new structure began to crumble around her. All that she'd
been striving to sustain and channel — her music, her
hopes, and her dreams — suddenly meant absolutely nothing to her. Her parents were gone. Nothing else was real.

For years, Sharon and Jerry had traveled Ontario's highways, both to earn a living and to support Shania's musical aspirations. Those roads were part of the pattern of their lives. That they should lose their lives because of a logging truck after fighting for years to make their reforestation business viable is a tragic irony. A recent change to Ontario law had also figured in the chain of events that resulted in the collision and contributed to the conviction that the Twains were in the worst possible place at the worst possible time. Shania explains: "We worked the forests planting trees in reforestation projects, from spring to fall each year. We did it for years as a family unit — then when the cold weather came, I'd go back to singing. It was on one of their last trips of the year that the accident happened — on a Sunday, not long after Sunday trucking was reintroduced on Ontario highways. It shouldn't have happened" (Delaney, "What Made Her").

Shock, denial, pain. From the welter of powerful emotions that were triggered by Jill's phone call, Shania emerged with the sense that she had to act decisively; she would refuse to succumb to the paralysis that accompanies despair. In retrospect, she describes her feelings like this: "It was like being thrown into the deep end of a pool and just having to swim" (Lague).

There were moments when the thought of having to pick up the pieces of her shattered family and fit them together again without a parent of her own to lean on was too much to bear, and her flight instinct kicked in. "I wanted to escape it all and go off to Africa," she remembers. "I wanted to get as far away as I could, somewhere where civilization was different, where I could escape everything that was happening. Either that or I was going to dig in and deal with it. I ended up staying and coping with the responsibility." So, ultimately, her

BARB BLANCHARD/DAN PORTER, COURTESY *COUNTRY MUSIC NEWS*

choice may have been predetermined: she'd been raised to face up to hardship — to deal with it. "After my parents died," she admits, "I didn't know what to do. All I knew was that I had to be there for my family" (Hager).

Shania quickly abandoned Toronto, the site of her new, independent existence, and retraced her steps to Timmins. She had a funeral to help arrange. It was a harrowing time, but the Twain children pulled together and got through it. Other family members, friends, and the community offered what support they could.

As all the activity died down and others resumed their daily lives, Shania and her siblings had to answer an urgent question: who would look after the youngest Twains? When Sharon and Jerry were killed, Shania's younger sister and her two brothers were still living at home. Carrie-Ann was eighteen, Mark was just fourteen, and Darryl was barely thirteen. Clearly, they could not manage on their own. Jill had left home ten years earlier and now had a family of her own to care for. She just wasn't in a position to take in three teenagers, and neither were members of the extended family. Foster care was unthinkable. That left Shania. "I was 22," she says, "there was no will, my brothers had no guardian because my younger sister was 18, and my older sister was married with children. So I simply assumed the role" (Keyes).

It was a huge personal sacrifice. At the very moment she had finally managed to position herself for flight, she was yanked back into the nest — and that nest required a lot of maintenance. Shania's social and professional lives vanished. She settled her parents' estate, educated herself about such arcane matters as death taxes, and guided three orphaned teenagers through their ordeal. "Having worked in the bush," she remarks, and "knowing all the contractors, I knew the value of my father's equipment, so I became the executrix of the estate. I sold it off, paid the bills, dealt with the taxes, the mortgage, everything" (Keyes).

Gradually, as life took on a more normal rhythm, Shania's thoughts returned to music. Others in her circumstances might have been tempted to pack everything in, give up their dream, take a steady day job, and consider themselves lucky if they could make ends meet. Shania, however, felt her resolve to become a professional entertainer resurface. It was evident, though, that she would have to develop a new approach, one that would accommodate her current setup. "I couldn't just go around getting gigs here and there or writing only when I felt like it," she says (Geocites). She believed she could make a decent living as a singer if she could only land the right job.

Shania turned to a close family friend, a woman who had mentored her since adolescence, for advice. It wasn't the first time, and it certainly wouldn't be the last, that Mary Bailey turned her attention to helping Shania clear an obstacle from her path. A "sturdy redhead with a welcoming smile" (Keyes), Mary Bailey had become, over the years, a source of support and inspiration for Shania. Mary offered a shoulder for her to cry on. She was one of the few non-Twains whom Shania felt she could completely trust. Furthermore, they shared a vocation: country music.

When Shania was a child performer, Mary was a relatively well-known country singer who had produced several small-scale hit singles. Like Shania, Mary was a rule-breaker, someone who pushed country music to its limits. Larry Delaney, editor of *Country Music News*, assesses her contribution: "You might even say Mary Bailey was playing New Country before New Country was even invented. She was something of a trailblazer" (conversation). If you listen to Mary's hit "Mystery Lady" (some fans began referring to her affectionately as "The Mystery Lady," and it seems she enjoyed it), you'll find it hard to disagree.

Why is it that so many fortuitous things have happened to Shania in mid-August? Mary and Shania first met just before Shania's birthday on 14 August 1978. Bailey comments, "she would only have been 12. I was performing in Sudbury, and she was the opening act. I was standing offstage when she sang [Hank Williams's] 'I'm So Lonesome I Could Cry,' and I was just blown away. She had the voice of a young Tanya Tucker. She was a great artist, even at that age" (Keyes). Mary introduced herself to Sharon Twain that night. They spoke, of course, about Sharon's remarkable young daughter, Eileen.

The late 1970s were lean times for Canadian country singers. These days, they are much more likely to be judged according to their own merits; then they were simply bush leaguers, wannabes, pale shadows of their "professional" American counterparts. On their own home turf, they could only hope to serve as warm-up acts for Nashville's touring bright lights. Mary Bailey had lived this reality for many years. She had persevered and proven her durability. She'd released a couple of singles with RCA, and she'd put out albums on her own label. In short, she was doing all right for a Canadian, and the best she could hope for was to remain in demand as an opener for those southern stars. When she finally encountered Sharon and Eileen Twain, she'd already started to think about retiring. Maybe the time had come for a career change.

That night in Sudbury, Shania's rendition of the Hank Williams classic had reduced Mary to tears. She had been mesmerized by the emotion in the little girl's powerful voice. Her own career was waning — she just didn't have it in her to keep it airborne anymore. Mary looked at Shania and saw the future. As she stood in the wings with Sharon, she talked to her about the potential she saw in Shania. The two women became friends, and as Shania grew, the bond between Sharon and Mary deepened. To Sharon, Mary was a veteran of the struggle her daughter was engaged in, and therefore a mine of information and wisdom. She turned to Mary frequently, soliciting her opinion on many of the career decisions that confronted her and Shania.

Mary, who was growing very fond of the child, was always happy to comply. She helped Sharon to decide which gigs to pursue and which contacts were worth developing. Their informal consultations worked well until Shania was on the brink of finishing high school. By this time, she had already attracted the attention of several would-be managers — she'd even been taken to Nashville in an attempt to attract some big-league interest, but nothing had come of it. Now Shania appeared to be altering her course and venturing into areas where Sharon and Mary couldn't follow.

Influenced by her friends, and by the heady sounds of the pervasive youth culture that encircled them all, Shania was straying from her country foundations. Pop and rock music had more cachet among people of her age group, and its allure could be irresistible. More and more of Shania's precious time was devoted to playing with rock bands. Sharon was worried. How could she guide her daughter's fledgling career and protect her from the sharp edges of the music business if Shania left the relatively safe, and certainly familiar, confines of country? Rock, to Sharon, was unknown — and therefore potentially treacherous — territory. She became convinced that

Shania needed real, focused, professional management. And Mary Bailey was the perfect person for the job. If Shania would have her, Mary was ready, willing, and able. It would be a fresh start for both of them.

Shortly after Shania graduated from Timmins High and Vocational, Mary became her manager. She had to buy out a management contract that Shania had signed earlier, but that contract had been a loose agreement and proved easy to take over. Mary believed that there was nothing Shania couldn't achieve with her assistance. Shania became her protégée. She herself was excited at the prospect of working with Bailey, and for awhile reset her sights on country. Mary took her back to Nashville, and together they made the rounds, but recording deals continued to elude them. They returned home empty-handed, and soon young Shania's commitment began to falter. Mary was forced to realize that Shania was still just too young, and her attraction to the glamorous trappings of the pop-rock world was both natural and uncontainable — at least for the time being. There were no hard feelings. Mary and Shania went their separate ways, wishing each other well, and promising to keep in touch.

That's how things stood when Shania was sent reeling by the death of her parents. Mary Bailey had remained the kind of friend you could count on in time of need, and Shania was in need. She asked Mary what she should do to provide for her younger siblings, and explained about the resurgence of her musical ambitions. Mary responded without hesitation, shoring up Shania's determination to resume her career in a more focused way. Shania recalls: "Mary said, 'You can't quit. I know this place. Come and see this show with me'" (Keyes).

Mary was able to see Shania's predicament with the objectivity of an outsider, but her love for Shania and her family also meant that she was sensitive to the magnitude of Shania's desperation. "You have great talent," she told Shania yet again, reassuring her that she was entirely capable of making a living as a singer and that her dream of a career in music had not perished with her mother and father (Leamer). The "place" Mary had mentioned was a famous old vacation resort in the heart of Ontario's cottage country. Located in Huntsville, about 150 miles north of Toronto, the upscale Deerhurst resort was then staging a nightly musical variety revue. The show was called Viva Vegas, and it drew relatively large crowds of tour-group members, corporate conventioneers, vacationers, and locals.

Mary pulled some strings and got Shania an audition with the Deerhurst producers. They were glad to have her but at first didn't know quite what to do with her. Lynn Foster, one of the Viva Vegas producers, explains: "At the time, we were not looking for a lead singer for the show. But after her audition and listening to her tape and actually having her perform in the lounge, we decided to make a spot for her. She was *that* good" (Newcomer). Shania didn't require any coaxing. "It seemed too good to be true. The salary was great, it was stationary, which would be good for Mark and Darryl, and I would probably learn things. I looked at it as a way of going to music college" (Keyes). It did, however, mean leaving Timmins. The family would have to set up housekeeping in Huntsville.

It took some cajoling, but Shania finally convinced "her kids" that moving would be the best course of action for everyone. She enrolled Darryl and Mark in a Huntsville school, rented a house just outside of town, and established their daily routine. For the next three years, she resolutely shouldered responsibilities that most women her age never even have to think about. She cooked, cleaned, managed the household budget, paid the bills, made sure the kids were well fed and generally healthy, went to parent-teacher meetings, shepherded the boys to teen dances, listened, and dispensed advice. At the same time, she rehearsed and performed six shows a week at Deerhurst. It was like holding down two full-time jobs. This period "was the hardest time of my life," Shania says. "[The kids] were teenagers and I was consumed by our lives. I escaped through my music" (Dunphy).

Her escape wasn't total, though — at Deerhurst, even though she had the gratifying sense of developing as a performer, she was working hard. "At the time you couldn't help but feel sorry for her," Foster remarks. She had taken on "quite a responsibility. She was a very focused — very professional, but very focused — individual. She had the responsibility of two younger brothers and a sister. So it didn't allow for a lot. She had aspirations and she knew she was going somewhere with her career. And she worked on it" (Newcomer).

If nothing else, Deerhurst was a career boot camp. And the training Shania got there would later prove invaluable. She worked as both a lounge singer and a performer in the glitzy Vegas-style revue. She was called upon to belt out tunes in a wide variety of musical styles. "When she performed in the lounge," Foster says, she "did Top 40 tunes. She went in there and she could really kick it" (Newcomer). Night after night, for three years, Shania sang everything from soft-rock hits to Andrew Lloyd Webber and Gershwin. In the revue, she covered the Village People's campy classic "YMCA" and crooned a Motown melody.

Clearly, the job was repetitive and confining. Shania was obliged to serve up other people's material to audiences who would have neither noticed nor cared if she was suddenly replaced by another prancing Vegas showgirl clone with a voice. Yet she considered it all an important experience. "It gave me a lot of confidence," she says. "I always had a dream of going to a performing arts school, and in some ways, that's what Deerhurst gave me" (Hager).

In fact, performing at the resort was generally a better experience for Shania than commanding center stage at (first) country-music bars and (later) rock clubs. "Deerhurst was more a theatre than a social bar," she elaborates, "so the audiences were much more attentive than what I'd had before." Still, she played to a mixed bag of folks at the resort — "One night it'd be all men, then foreign tourists, then an all-women convention, whatever" — and therefore learned exactly what it took to grab and hold the attention of a diverse group of people, how to drag them away from their drinks and food and conversation and actually make them listen (Keyes).

"In that particular show," says Lynn Foster, "Shania had a big ballad, a combination of 'Somewhere out There' and 'Over the Rainbow.' That always got a fabulous reaction. It was a great combination of two songs — a really pretty ballad. She wore this beautiful green gown, and she's a very attractive lady. That was a knockout number" (Newcomer). Being so young and attractive, it was inevitable that she would impress a few patrons for the wrong reasons. In this regard, Deerhurst again turned out to be an excellent training ground. Shania soon learned how to deflect the advances of assorted drunks and lechers swiftly and tactfully. It was all in a day's work.

Shania's second full-time job, that of surrogate mom, was more difficult to master. It was brutal. She was run ragged trying to hold everything together. Just when the

Twain collective had finally settled into its new life, the well literally ran dry. Suddenly, there was no water. Shania recollects: "We would bathe in the river, and then I would do the laundry. I kept watching for cars, thinking, 'I'm gonna get arrested.' Then I bought a house — a small house, 900-or-something square feet, and that well went dry. We went down to the river with five-gallon jugs, that's how we'd flush the toilets. No different from a lot of people at their cottage, I guess. Listen, I was afraid to do the wrong thing. I was just a kid of 22. I wasn't doing a great job, but I was doing the right thing. Nobody helped me out, but I never felt needy" (Keyes).

Slowly, the situation eased a little. Shania fixed up her house and bought a truck, and she and her siblings finally managed to attain some stability. Shania was maturing into a remarkably poised and self-reliant young woman. The respect and love her brothers had for her deepened, despite some moments of conflict — of the willful teen versus the strong-minded surrogate parent variety. Mark Twain asserts that, overall, Shania was a great parent. He also says that he now understands why she was sometimes so hard on them: "She was really strict with us. She was scared" (Lague). Shania, however, has credited her brothers with keeping her strong. And though she does admit to being a little hard on them, in the end she's confident that her intentions were always good. "They were going through so much," she says, "I was just concerned about them" (Keyes).

During those three years in Huntsville, the Twain children's wounds began to heal. Not a day went by that they didn't miss their parents, but for the most part they were happy. By 1991, the boys had finished high school and were ready to move out on their own. Shania was liberated, and it felt wonderful. "When they left," she confides,

"I felt like a 45-year-old woman whose kids had gone away to college. I was like *'Wow!'* I have my whole life to live now. I had all this time on my hands. I didn't have to cook and clean for anybody. Didn't have to pay any bills but mine. Didn't have to go to school meetings. Didn't have to pick them up after work and take them to dances. Drive 'em here. Drive 'em there. It was like 'I'm *free!*' I said 'now what am I gonna do with my life?' I decided I wanted to go for it!" (Press Release).

COURTESY BILL BORGWARDT

Going for it meant calling on Mary Bailey once more. Shania had come to the conclusion that country was her calling, and if she was going to broach the country-music world again, she wanted Mary by her side, as her manager. Shania explains "I told [Mary] I was ready to give it my everything, could she please see what might be available to me" (Delaney, "What Made Her"). Bailey, of course, agreed to help. With Mary guiding her, Shania embarked on the trajectory that would lead her to the pot of gold: the career she enjoys today. The first step was to quit Deerhurst and return to Timmins. There she would focus exclusively on building her country-music act. To keep her body and soul together during this interval, she took a job at the complaint desk in the Timmins outlet of Sears.

The Huntsville-Deerhurst chapter of her life was relegated to memory.

★ ★ ★

In 1996, still flying high on the success of *The Woman in Me*, Shania snuck back to Deerhurst. "She wanted to surprise me and the cast," says Foster, "so she didn't tell me that she was coming. Actually, it was kind of neat. She didn't want to be acknowledged. Obviously, there were some people in the room who knew she was there. But most people just left her alone to enjoy the evening with her family. And, of course, she had a visit with all the cast." Watching the show, Shania became aware of some interesting changes in the lineup. For one thing, the country component had expanded. No fewer than four Shania Twain numbers had been added. Foster remarks, "I said to her afterwards, 'Did you ever think that one day we would be doing *your* songs on this stage?' I think she got a real kick out of it" (Newcomer).

From her three-year adventure-ordeal, Shania gleaned a series of experiences that would both shape her life and inspire her music. The surrogate-parent experience, for example, evoked in her some strong black-and-white attitudes towards child-rearing. Today she expresses her determination to instill basic, no-nonsense values in the children she and Mutt plan to have at some point: "I'd like to teach my kids to get by on as little as possible. In retrospect, you know, I was never desperate. Going down to the river [for water] didn't depress me. I'd been through so much as a kid. Clothes? So what! Sleeping on the floor? So what! Washing in the river? So what! — you're not going to die" (Keyes).

Coming out of the Huntsville-Deerhurst years, Shania made an even more vital discovery. Her wealth of experience was starting to coalesce with her creative capacity; what she had seen and endured had begun to work its way into the songs she had jangling around inside her head. Her own unique blend of sounds, her own unique form of country, was taking shape. In fact, she started to compose one of the most startlingly tender tracks on *The Woman in Me* during this time: the gospel-tinged "God Bless the Child." "It is good the way it is," Shania now comments. It "is not really a complete song. What it is, is a musical thought, an expression. At the time, when my parents died, what that lullaby did for me was to comfort me. It soothed me. It was like a bellow of sorrow. I would go for long walks and just sing this" (Brown).

Finally, this trying period yielded her name. She and Mary concluded that "Eileen" just wouldn't work on a marquee. There was a Native woman who worked as a wardrobe assistant at Deerhurst, Eileen ventured, and she had a beautiful Ojibwa name. It meant "I'm on my way." Maybe that would be a good choice. Mary Bailey asked her protégée what the name was. "Shania," she said.

TONY MOTTRAM/RETNA

6

DANCE WITH THE ONE THAT BROUGHT YOU

What's in a name? In Shania's case, a lot. From the moment Eileen Twain was eclipsed by Shania, the woman who embodied them both was, at last, on her way. It was 1991, the year of her rebirth. Shania reentered the world of country music equipped with little more than her vocal talent, her songwriting ability, and a renewed faith in the viability of her dreams. And there were two other things. She also had her extraordinary life experience and an impressive professional track record. These merged to spark in her the confidence that she had, despite what any of her detractors would later say, paid her dues. By this point, Shania had performed more than a thousand times; still in her twenties, she was a seasoned pro.

Starting from scratch like this could have been extremely disheartening. It could have prompted feelings of regret over time wasted. Shania would not permit herself to fall into this particular trap. Entertaining such negative thoughts at this crucial juncture would have been like stepping into quicksand. As far as Shania was concerned, the universe was unfolding as it should.

Shania is a Virgo. This may sound like a trivial observation, but it's amazing how closely Shania's personality traits conform to those that make up the profile of the typical Virgo. And those traits all seem to have come to the fore as Eileen metamorphosed into Shania. People born between 23 August and 22 September are usually adaptable, intelligent, and extremely creative. They make dutiful partners, and they cherish family: in fact, family is often their major source of pride and joy. Because they tend to be fiercely independent, they also require some solitude, some time and space to recharge their batteries. Virgos have the capacity to remain relatively serene, despite external pressures. Whenever their characters are put to the test, they stay cool, calm, and collected; rational people, they adjust their lives to effect a solution to a problem. Virgos are survivors. Adaptive strength and resilience are among their dominant traits.

Those born under the influence of this sign are able, when necessary, to follow their heads and not their hearts — in their world, logic often prevails over emotional considerations. Some consider Virgos cold and calculating. But while they can make what seem to be rather cold-blooded decisions, they do so only when threatened by something. Virgos display grace under pressure. Similarly, in their professional lives they are often clear-headed; they manifest an I'll-believe-it-when-I-see-it, show-me-the-money kind of attitude. Virgos are loyal people who have little use for hearsay — they want to make decisions based on fact, not faith.

Shania fits the bill. She craved solitude when she was growing up, and felt at home in the lonely northern bush; her family loyalty and her creative independence are equally fierce; her response to the ordeal of childhood poverty was philosophical and practical; she adapted calmly to the death of her parents, and coped with the pressures that tragedy brought to bear on her life with grace. Entering the 1990s equipped with all these traits, Shania, a clear-headed Virgo, was ready to put her creativity to its ultimate challenge. She was finally ready to make a life for herself on her own terms, a life that would be determined by her talent, her music.

When it came to formulating the business plan, Mary Bailey would step in. Mary had long been convinced that Shania's return to country was inevitable. "She was raised on it," Mary says matter-of-factly, "and she moved away from it, as young people do. But she's very 'rootsy'" (Keyes). Now, in the early 1990s, Mary could see that Shania's youthful enthusiasm, energy, and "rootsiness" had come together in a mature, professional package: she was no longer too young. It was time for Shania to strike while the proverbial iron was hot. So, after the pair had selected Shania's new name, and while Shania dismantled her life in Huntsville and made arrangements to return to Timmins, where she would work at honing her best country chops, they began to work on a strategy that would make Nashville sit up and take notice.

As they worked, their professional maneuverings were empowered by the dynamics of their personal relationship. Shania, coming out of three years of surrogate mothering, now found herself under the wing of her own surrogate mother. Mary, in being asked to involve herself in Shania's future, felt doubly blessed: not only was she given the opportunity to shepherd the "daughter" she'd thought she'd never have (although she was married and had a son), but she was also given a chance to realize her own career aspirations vicariously through a young performer with amazing drive and talent. She wasn't trying to reinvent herself in her protégée, she wasn't going through a midlife crisis, and she wasn't chasing after her own youth. Mary was merely seizing the day: here was a once-in-a-lifetime chance to help a loved one, work at something she enjoyed, and maintain a foothold in a world that had always fascinated her. And, having been through so much as a performer, having acquired an intimate knowledge of the vicissitudes of the business, having accumulated a valuable contact list over the years, Mary was just what Shania needed. The partnership was, in a word, well-balanced.

As a manager, Mary lacked some of the business acumen and savvy of many of the more high-profile — often cutthroat — Nashville players, but she more than made up for this deficiency with her heart and her tenacity. Furthermore, because Mary loved Shania and believed in her so passionately, she lavished on her the kind of support and attention that no other professional manager would have been willing to give such an unproven commodity. Mary became so emotionally invested in Shania's career that each time her young client stepped out onto a stage she felt she was on the line, too.

Throughout the early 1990s, the two women were inseparable. They were co-conspirators, a tireless and harmonious team — the unknown performer and her relatively unknown champion. Without Mary, Shania may never have made it to where she is today. It would be a mistake to downplay Mary's importance. As Larry Delaney remarks, Mary Bailey "was the perfect person, in the right place at the right time" (conversation). But it wasn't just Mary's energy and know-how that launched Shania: her money also paved the way.

Like running for public office, making a bid for success in the music business can be a risky and expensive undertaking. Having northern Ontario as your home

GLENN WEINER/SHOOTING STAR

base when the object of your campaign is in Tennessee adds significantly to the cost. Shania could never have paid for the necessities of her new venture with her Sears salary and what she made from the occasional gig alone. So Mary Bailey put up the cash, and the pair used it as efficiently as they could to get Shania noticed by all the right people. Mary's son, Robert Kasner, comments, "My dad was making his money and my mom was spending it on this dream. Everything had to be perfect before she went out with Shania" (Leamer). While this may have been a source of bitter feelings within Mary's nuclear family in the short term, later on it became apparent that Mary's infusion of cash into Shania's career would yield huge dividends.

As Shania tied up loose ends in Huntsville, she also compiled a demo tape of original music. She had a good deal of material by this time, some of it still quite raw. Not one to sit twiddling her thumbs, either, Mary was already hard at work as Shania's manager. She put out the word that Shania was returning to country and began networking. In the course of her own career, she'd developed a reputation as a straight shooter and initiated relationships with a range of Nashville insiders; a lot of them were still very fond of the red-headed "mystery lady." They valued her integrity and her professional opinion, and many considered her a friend. Among this coterie of longtime associates and friends was Richard Frank, an attorney who specialized in entertainment law. Frank was one of the founders of the influential Country Music Association, and was renowned within the Nashville music community as someone with an eye and an ear for talent. Mary Bailey's enthusiasm about her new client sparked his interest, and he agreed to give Shania's demo a listen.

Frank was impressed enough with what he heard to travel all the way to Canada to see Shania perform live. Right off the bat, then, Shania was not going about things the Nashville way: instead of taking her act to Music City and courting Frank, she obliged this music-industry emissary to trek north to her home territory. Shania was approaching the end of her Deerhurst tenure when Mary reeled in Frank, and so it was arranged that he and his wife, escorted by Mary, would catch Shania at that venue. Frank was hooked. He left Huntsville promising to do whatever he could for this beautiful tower of power packed into a five-foot-two-inch frame. True to his word, when he returned to Nashville, he got on the phone. And when Frank talked, people listened. The buzz had started. Word on the street was that this new girl from Canada was good — very good. In Shania's own words, "it became a chain reaction" (Delaney, "What Made Her").

When Shania recounts the events that led up to the release of *Shania Twain*, she tends to sound a little breathless. It's not surprising. From this point on, things started to move very quickly. Frank, in Shania's words, "got the ball rolling, setting up a meeting with producer Norro Wilson. He introduced me to Buddy Cannon, who was in A&R at Mercury Nashville at the time, and he handed my tape over to the head of the label. That was it!" (Geocites).

On the strength of Frank's good word, Mary was able to arrange a meeting between her, Shania, and Norro Wilson, one of Nashville's top independent producers. Wilson had been a fixture of the Music City scene since the late 1950s, and he, too, knew a good thing when it crossed his path. Like Mary, Wilson had started out as a performer. Later, he became a professional songwriter, supplying some of Nashville's more successful acts with solid material. By the 1990s, he had worked his way into the technical side of the business and was a highly respected free agent. The threesome hit it off, and Wilson became excited at the prospect of working with Shania. He felt, however, that her demo didn't quite cut it, that she needed a more polished product to present to the major labels. Again, Mary had to foot the bill; she covered Shania's travel expenses and paid Norro Wilson to record three of her songs.

It was major wish-fulfillment time. At long last, Shania was in a Nashville recording studio, cutting her own tunes, and acting as lead singer. Her days of supplying backup vocals and taking a walk-on part in someone else's dream seemed to be over. The three sides Wilson cut showcased Shania's range. Armed with the tape, and confident that it displayed Shania to her best advantage, Wilson lined up several Mercury Nashville reps, including Buddy Cannon, and requested that they give the work their serious consideration.

When Mercury president Luke Lewis finally heard the tape, everything fell into place. In late 1991, Shania signed her first Nashville recording contract and became Mercury Nashville's newest up-and-comer. The label was committed to sustaining the momentum, and so it quickly hired Wilson to produce Shania's debut album. Wilson, though, would not be overseeing the project alone: as coproducer, Mercury recruited one of its top executives, Harold Shedd; he was also the man who'd signed Shania.

What a year. Shania had gone from being a struggling young substitute mother working six nights a week in an attempt to support her charges to landing a recording contract with a major Nashville label. Talking to *Interview* magazine in 1996, Shania downplayed the drama of her near-miraculous ascent: "It was remarkably smooth. I didn't have to spend five years banging on doors in Nashville to be heard. There must have just been a space for me" (Powell). Such comments do little to put the enormous and extended effort she and Mary had exerted to get that far into perspective. Shania's overnight success was really a product of no less than two decades of apprenticeship. In 1992, Shania was installed in Nashville's Music Mill recording studio and singing her heart out for posterity. She was still shuttling back and forth between Timmins and Music City, but now there was no time for boredom to creep in behind the complaint desk at Sears.

As the preparations for her first release progressed, however, it became clear that Shania would have to establish a temporary residence where the action was. This geographic shift, like so many of the other radical changes she was going through, played havoc with her personal life. For one thing, Shania had begun seeing Paul Bolduc, a native of Timmins, and her changes of address were putting their relationship under stress. Paul elected to follow Shania to Nashville and try to make things cohere. He and his entire family had actually numbered among Shania's earliest and strongest supporters. Paul's mother, Hélène, would help found the Canadian chapter of the Shania Twain Fan Club. For many years, the club's offices were located in the basement of the Bolducs' white frame house. The Bolducs were Shania's dear friends; they came to treat her as if she were already a part of their family. Hélène had hoped to become her mother-in-law one day.

Marriage, however, was not in the cards for Paul and Shania. And though Shania included a special thank-you to Paul on the insert sleeve of *Shania Twain*, referring to him as her "saving grace," the rapidly accelerating demands of her career hobbled their relationship, and they finally broke up. Hélène insists that there weren't too many hard feelings. It was just one of those things. And despite the breakup, she continued her work with the fan club. "What was between me and Shania was real," Hélène says. Shania and Paul breaking up "didn't change anything. It wasn't easy but life goes on." Shania even asked Hélène to attend her wedding. This may seem odd or inappropriate given the circumstances, but it had been a tough call for Shania: Hélène and her family had done so much for her, and Shania wanted to return the favor by including Hélène in one of her most important rites of passage. Hélène acknowledges the gesture. "I was invited," she says, "but I couldn't do that to Paul" (Dunphy).

Personal turmoil aside, Shania's professional life, now centered in Nashville, was progressing smoothly. Once the record deal was signed, Norro Wilson sat down with Shania and Mary to decide which songs Shania should cover. Wilson was old school. He didn't have enough faith in Shania's songwriting skills to feel comfortable committing her material to disc. Like so many country-music people, he believed in doing things the traditional way, and that meant promoting Shania on the basis of her vocal talent. His attitude was, leave the songwriting to the professionals. In the wake of *The Woman in Me*, with its string of Shania-composed megahits, it's obvious that Wilson made a serious error in judgment.

From the vast reserve of material produced by Music City writers over the decades, they culled nine tracks that Wilson felt would effectively represent the range of his new sensation. As a concession to Shania and Mary, he also agreed to include one original Shania Twain composition, the catchy "God Ain't Gonna Getcha for That." And so, supported by a crew of seasoned session players, Shania made her debut album. The cuts were recorded and mixed by Jim Cotton and Joe Scaife under the watchful eyes of coproducers Shedd and Wilson. Shania's vocals were clear and powerful, at times haunting and at times provocative. The instrumentation, too, was rock solid. Cotton and Scaife used the studio talent to its fullest potential.

But before all the details for Shania's debut were finalized, even before the album's ten tracks had been completely mastered by Hank Williams at Mastermix and the Virginia Team design group had laid out the photos from the Timmins "wolf" shoot, the brain trust at Mercury had shifted into high gear. Mercury wanted to devise some strategies to give Shania and a couple of other young newcomers a head start. Because the label understood how important it is for emerging artists to gain exposure, to attain some level of public recognition as a preliminary step to developing a loyal fan base, it had earned a reputation as a country-music innovator.

Just a year earlier, for example, it had made music-biz history with Billy Ray Cyrus before his first record had even come out. Mercury released his first single, "Achy Breaky Heart," as a promotional video. Launching an act, in this case a gyrating Billy Ray, onto the country-music scene via video was an unprecedented move for a Nashville label. It worked brilliantly. Cyrus was practically a household name before people could get their hands on his album. Mercury A&R (or research and development) man Buddy Cannon, Harold Shedd, and label president Luke Lewis felt that Shania was a good candidate for the same procedure.

So it was decided. "What Made You Say That" would be the vehicle to introduce Shania to the public and to the media. Only this time, Mercury wouldn't rely on video alone. The first step was to team Shania with two other new artists from its stable: John Brannen and Toby Keith. They formed what Mercury promotions people dubbed the "Triple Play," and the advertising campaign designed to get the ball rolling relied heavily on the baseball motif: these were "Three Home Run Artists." Each singer was about to release an album, so several tracks were taken from each of their works and packaged together on a CD sampler. The artwork featured the trio standing together and flashing megawatt smiles at their future audiences. A similarly packaged promotional video also made the rounds, and Mercury pushed hard to get both radio and television airtime for their new talent. Unfortunately, it's not always possible to reproduce a winning formula. The Billy Ray Cyrus miracle did not occur all over again. At best, the Triple Play promotion gave Brannen, Keith, and Shania an edge over other new country artists who had spring releases.

Shania was thrilled with all the attention. Her debut album wasn't due until the third week of April, yet by March her name, face, and music had already started to crop up regularly in some of country's most influential print and electronic media outlets. People were starting to talk about the girl from Timmins, and Mary Bailey's phone lines lit up. Everybody, it seemed, wanted to know more about Shania Twain.

At the same time, word of Shania's vocal skills had spread within the Nashville recording community. A few of the calls Mary fielded were from other artists and producers eager to work with this fresh talent. A flattered Shania was happy to oblige. Jeff Chance's 1992 album *Walk Softly on the Bridges* featured Shania backup vocals on three cuts: "Touching Home," "Where Do I Go from Here," and the title track. Then, in early 1993, Shania made a big splash by guesting on Sammy Kershaw's hit album

RON WOLFSON/LONDON FEATURES

Haunted Heart — she harmonized on the singles "Still Lovin' You" and "What Might Have Been."

In the meantime, Shania's sexy video of "What Made You Say That," part of the Triple Play promo package, was making waves. Filmed in Miami Beach, it featured what Mercury judged were her two greatest assets: her powerful, expressive voice and her extraordinary good looks. The clip isn't really much more than three minutes of Shania cavorting by the ocean with a shirtless hunk, but it turned a lot of heads. "What Made You Say That" is an uptempo, bouncy little number penned by Tony Haselden and Stan Munsey Jr., but lyrically the track is pretty standard country fare. It's an infectious, irreverent, "Wow, I'm really in love" kind of song, but it does feature a beguiling blend of indecision and sass and permits Shania's polished vocal delivery to shine forth.

The "What Made You Say That" video and the *Triple Play* sampler represented a substantial investment in an untried performer. Even so, Mercury's prerelease push for *Shania Twain* was still not complete. The label booked its three new hitters — Shania, Brannen, and Keith — on a whirlwind sixteen-city tour. The pace was furious now, but Shania refused to let it go to her head. Struggling to keep her eyes on the road as she entered the fast lane, she gave thanks to a higher power for guiding her to success: "I feel so lucky, after going through such sadness when we lost mom and dad. It seems like God has been watching over me and helping me every step of the way. He took something precious away . . . now He's giving me something special. I guess it's all part of the 'overall' plan he has for us" (Delaney, "What Made Her").

In retrospect, the Triple Play tour proved to be both a positive and a negative undertaking. The emphasis, unfortunately, was on the latter. On the upside, Shania had everything to gain from the exposure to new audiences the tour brought her, and from the opportunity to fine-tune her stage presence in a country milieu. On the downside, she often felt like the tour "outsider," and it took her awhile to adjust to performing for crowds who'd been raised on a steady diet of American country (Richmond).

But it gets worse than that. When all was said and done, Shania, Brannen, and even Mercury Nashville had precious little to show for their efforts. The only one who came away from the experience unequivocally better off was Toby Keith: he tucked a hit album under his belt. The tour was a logistical nightmare (try maneuvering just *one* act through a sixteen-stop marathon), and pitted performer against performer. Competing with all the other country hopefuls who had imminent major-label releases, dealing with the unrealistic expectations of industry players who were desperately seeking the next Billy Ray, contending with the successes, failures, and insecurities of your own label mates — whose fortunes had been arbitrarily linked to your own — at close range: it was a recipe for frustration and tension. After all, Brannen, Keith, and Shania were fighting for the biggest piece of the same pie. And, having waited so many years for this, the chance of a lifetime, who could blame them for not wanting to share?

Shania had no time to go home and brood after that essentially ill-fated tour. Her album hit the stands, and almost every waking moment for the following three months was booked. On the heels of the Triple Play circus came a Canadian radio and TV promo tour. Meet-and-greet events were scheduled across America in May. Early June was dedicated to occupying a booth and performing at the mega-important Nashville Fan Fair. From there,

Shania would travel to a base in Little Rock, Arkansas, where she would entertain ten thousand troops by special request. Then it would be time to shoot a video for her follow-up single.

In personal terms, at least, *Shania Twain* represented a huge leap forward and had to be considered a success. Shortly after the album was released, Shania voiced her sole regret on that score: "Only that Music City U.S.A. is not somewhere in Northern Ontario. I get lonely for family and friends in Timmins and Huntsville, and miss the bush and not being able to jump in my truck and get lost in the woods. But I love it here, and I know that if I want to 'make it' in country music I have to do it from Nashville. Most singers in Canada would give an arm and a leg for what I've got going . . . so I guess I'd better not complain about being lonely!" (Delaney, "What Made Her"). Professionally, however, it came down to this: *Shania Twain* had not yielded a hit song.

Neither Shania nor Mary has ever expressed her disappointment with the record publicly. Neither have they sacrificed any opportunity to promote *Shania Twain* or put the best possible spin on what it did achieve. But both women must have known that one critic's assessment of the record wasn't too far off the mark: *Shania Twain* is "a generic collection of country tunes by other writers" that "created little excitement" (Jennings). Sales were poor. The first single, "What Made You Say That," peaked at number fifty-five on the *Billboard* country-music charts, and without the engine of a hit single the album only managed to sell a little over a hundred thousand copies worldwide. It made some inroads in certain American markets — Denver, Salt Lake City, and Seattle — but that just wasn't good enough.

It was kind of scary. If something didn't break for Shania

soon, it would be quite a trick for Mary to find someone to pay for her second kick at the can. Then fortune smiled. Two phone calls lifted Shania out of the doldrums and set her back on track. Both calls came from men who did not have strong ties to Nashville, and both were responses to the "What Made You Say That" video. When the first came in, Mary didn't recognize the caller's name. It would have stunned her to know then that the voice on the other end of the line belonged to the man who would utterly transform Shania's professional life. Not to mention her personal one.

"Mutt" Lange is among the most respected producers in the music business. Acts as astonishingly diverse as Def Leppard, AC/DC, Bryan Adams, Foreigner, Billy Ocean, and Michael Bolton have flourished under his influence. Lange himself was a hot commodity, and when he called an artist's manager, he could expect to be granted an attentive audience. In the spring of 1993, he was working out to a new video that a friend had given him. After a while, he realized that he had come to a complete stand-still; he'd stopped exercising and was looking and listening intently. Shania was there before him, belting out "What Made You Say That," and Lange was intrigued.

He had to talk to her. She was beautiful, she could sing, and she was loaded with potential. He could help her, he was convinced, to become a superstar. Mercury put Lange onto Mary Bailey; the rest should have been history — but it wasn't. Mary had no idea who this keener with the English accent could be, and she concluded that he was yet another intrepid, cold-calling fan. Shania hadn't a clue who he was either, so they sent poor Mutt an autographed publicity photo and expected never to hear from him again. They were very lucky. Instead of taking offence, Mutt was charmed by their innocent brush-off. If he'd had a bigger ego and a smaller sense of humor, *The Woman in Me* would never have been born.

The second caller suffered no such treatment. Mary had no doubts about whom she was dealing with this time: it was actor-director Sean Penn calling from Hollywood. Penn, like Lange, had been blown away by Shania in the "What Made You Say That" video. Would Shania, he asked Mary, be interested in having him help produce her next video? The answer, of course, was a resounding "Yes!" "It was a total thrill," Shania says. "I was jumping up and down when I found out he was interested in doing my video." It was the kind of opportunity that rarely lands on the doorstep of a country artist. Shania knew it, and she was not going to blow this chance. "There are some things you can anticipate," she remarks. "I certainly anticipated a recording contract, because that was what I was working toward for many years. But working with Sean Penn was totally unexpected" (Chodan, "Shania Twain Goes").

Mercury had been planning to do a second Shania Twain video, for the song "Dance with the One That Brought You," as a means of giving her languishing album one last promotional shove. Penn was brought in as soon as he could make himself available, and he immediately took control of the project. Filming got under way in mid-May with actor Charles Durning playing Shania's "goodtime Charlie" love interest. The song itself, written by Sam Hogin and Gretchen Peters, is a midtempo number featuring some nice slide-guitar work and a catchy, anthemlike chorus; the lyrics are a list of standard tips on how to keep your man once you've snared him — the kind of thing that you might find in a back issue of *Cosmo*.

While the song was an adequate vehicle for Shania's vocal talents, it failed — as did "What Made You Say That"

— to allow her unique personality to shine through. Ultimately, neither of Shania's first two video-supported singles was distinctive enough to rise above the tide of freshly issued tunes and achieve hit status. Penn or no Penn. What Penn did do for Shania, however, was teach her a few things about acting, and this — when, in a couple of years' time, she had better material to work with — would prove extremely useful. Shania's two-and-a-half-minute performance for the "Dance" video was actually so promising that Penn encouraged her to try her hand at acting on the big screen. Would Shania ever consider trying her luck in Hollywood? These days, the buzz is that she's (as they say in the business) "just waiting for the right project to come along."

The third single and video release from *Shania Twain*, the ballad "You Lay a Whole Lot of Love on Me," fared no better than the first two. It was essentially a pop-country ballad, the kind of tune that a vocalist like Anne Murray has interpreted to perfection so many times. Yet, once again, Shania was confined by the limitations of someone else's material. Written in 1979 by Forest Borders and Hank Beach, "You Lay a Whole Lot of Love on Me" was just too syrupy for the 1990s country market. The chorus was recorded with a male voice ghosting Shania's; the effect is haunting, and the ballad as a whole does highlight her gorgeous voice, but in the end it's the kind of song that promises something it can't deliver.

Listen to the rest of *Shania Twain*, particularly in light of what was to follow, and you'll get a strong sense of an artist being held back by her material. Shania can't cut loose here, and because of this it seems as though her heart's not really in it. This is an inoffensive, laid-back, almost reserved record. Take even the most energetic numbers — songs like the funky, I'm-not-gonna-take-any-

Shania at homecoming in Timmins, 1996

RACHELE LABRECQUE

Homecoming, Timmins, 1996

RACHELE LABRECQUE

more-of-your-crap anthem "Forget Me," the rollicking and irreverent "Crime of the Century," or the bluesy, bass-heavy "Got a Hold on Me" (though its smoky, sultry vocal track makes it one of the album's most appealing tunes). They all leave you feeling that Shania has been fettered by production techniques intended to make her as listener-friendly as possible. The album's ballads also fall short of the mark. Although the tempo of the songs is so consistent — understated and easy — the album does allow Shania a little latitude to explore a few lyrical and thematic styles. "Still under the Weather," for example, is a passable hurting song, with just the right "what doesn't kill you only makes you stronger" sentiment, while "When He Leaves You" is a functional "my cheating man" lament. "There Goes the Neighborhood" is Shania's vehicle to try her hand at interpreting a country standby: the story song. She pulls it off with the requisite amount of emotional honesty.

The brightest light on *Shania Twain* is the one song that she wrote herself: the wry, engaging, honky-tonk smoker "God Ain't Gonna Getcha for That." It's lyrically flirtatious, a little provocative, and Shania puts it across with everything she's got. Not even the album's middle-of-the-road production could hold her back. Here, more than anywhere else on Shania's debut album, you can discern the seed that would blossom into *The Woman in Me*.

Video has been absolutely crucial to Shania's ascent to superstardom. The single tangible indicator of the success *Shania Twain* would receive was a direct result of the mini-movies she had made to promote the album. This signal of recognition derived from neither Canada nor the U.S. Instead, in 1993, Shania picked up the first of the many awards she would soon collect from, of all places,

Europe. In fact, when Country Music Television Europe awarded her its Rising Star Award based on the *Shania Twain* videos, the honor went a long way towards salvaging the whole debut-album debacle for both Shania and Mary. And for Mercury Nashville. The award communicated to fickle Nashville executives that there was still hope for the girl from Timmins, Ontario.

Buoyed by this testimonial to Shania's capacity to appeal to a mass audience, industry movers and shakers refrained, for the time being, from suggesting that she should pack it in. In her first "Fan Letter" contribution to Canada's *Country* magazine, Shania readily acknowledged in 1994 that the video networks had become her lifeline to the fans and, therefore, a career saver: "Country Music Television has been extremely helpful to me this past year in giving me visibility throughout North America and Europe. I actually won my first award from CMT Europe . . . VH1, MuchMusic and TNN have also been incredibly helpful." This was something of an understatement. These powerful networks were more than just helpful. They had, in fact, become an integral part of Shania's overall marketing strategy.

As had the idea of making personal contact with "real" people — individuals who could be added to Shania's fan base. With the release of *Shania Twain*, Shania had learned all about the benefits to be reaped from making personal appearances. So she undertook to meet and greet, and in time she developed the routine into one of the most important factors behind the success of *The Woman in Me*. Shaking hands with fans, smiling at them, posing for their photos, and just chatting — it all seemed to come naturally to Shania. And if *Shania Twain* was not going to spawn a hit single to do the work for her, she was going to sell her debut CD one copy at a time. Her personal charm, of course, went a long way towards making this possible: if anybody could make an album a success using this unlikely strategy, it was Shania.

Needless to say, therefore, when Mercury and Mary Bailey arranged for Shania to have a booth at the annual Nashville Fan Fair in June, she was ready. Even eager. The Fan Fair is a key event for every country performer simply because of the sheer number of people who attend it. It represents a golden opportunity to reach out and touch countless record buyers — and to find out, first hand, what they want to hear.

The 1993 Nashville Fan Fair was an enormously significant one for Shania. Here she met one particular fan who, perhaps better than anyone else in the music business, knew what all the other fans wanted from an artist. It was Mutt Lange. By now, he had persuaded Mary to put him in touch with Shania herself, and the two had embarked on a telephone relationship based on Shania's music, but they had never actually seen one another. At the Fan Fair, they finally met face to face.

★ ★ ★

With the release of *Shania Twain*, Mary Bailey completed the project she had undertaken just two years earlier. She had guided Shania's career further, in that short period of time, than either woman had dared hope. It had truly been an astounding ascent. As a team, the two had realized their mutual dream: they had staked out a position in Nashville, and they were playing the game.

But when Shania came together with Mutt, she knew she had found the missing piece to her career puzzle; she had hit a brick wall, and Mutt had the skill and the muscle to pull her over the top and set her back on course. Lange could escort her to superstardom. Mary, of course, was

still her closest female friend and confidante, and she
would go on to fulfill a major role in marketing *The
Woman in Me*. In September 1995, when Shania collected
the first of many major awards for her second album, a
Female Artist of the Year trophy at the Canadian Country
Music Awards ceremony in Hamilton, Ontario, Mary sat
next to the honoree in the audience and wept with joy
as Shania's name was announced. A television camera held
Mary in a tight close-up as Shania was accepting the
award. It was a wonderful moment, a flash of public
recognition for their joint accomplishment. Mary's son,
Robert Kasner, told the *Toronto Star* that at the time
everything at last seemed perfect: Mary had negotiated
the ups and downs and triumphed over the odds. "That's
what we thought," he said. "But that seems to have
escaped Shania's memory" (Dunphy). It hasn't, though,
and it's unlikely that it will.

What irks Kasner is the decision Shania was forced
to make at this crossroads in her career. Lange, with *The
Woman in Me*, had produced an artistic, critical, and
popular sensation the dimensions of which stunned
everyone in the business — including Shania and Mary.
Shania was therefore confronted with a heartbreaking
dilemma: she wanted to go on, she wanted to dance with
the one who had brought her into the stratosphere, but
how could she fit Mary into these plans? So she ration-
alized: "Change is normal . . . I like to go forward.
I'm not a stand-still kind of person. I don't get caught in
a comfort zone" (Leamer). Still, sometimes change is
wrenching; sometimes it exacts a huge personal toll.

Yet any objective observer with a little knowledge of
the music business would be inclined to render the same
judgment: Shania's career had gotten too big for Mary
Bailey to manage. Case closed. Mary had to go. And

though it hurt her terribly, Shania was fully capable of acting on this brutal logic in Virgo-like fashion. She had to take a highly charged personal situation and defuse it, depersonalize it, by employing her business sense. John Landau and Barbara Carr, Bruce Springsteen's management team, eventually became Shania's new handlers. It took a while — a significant amount of time elapsed between the firing of Mary and the hiring of Landau and Carr — but Shania insisted on weighing her options carefully. The split with Mary had been traumatic, and Shania hadn't put them both through it just to replace her beloved mentor with management that was anything less then stellar.

When she publicly announced her decision to go with Landau and Carr in the fall of 1996, Shania commented on how trying the entire process had been, but she also argued that it had been unavoidable. "I was determined to take a break and decide what it is I really need in a manager, what is going to just make it all come together, which is what a manager does," she said. "I'm not the easiest person to manage because I'm independent. If I could manage myself I would but it's just more than I can handle. I want to focus on the music and the creative end of things but I'll always want to be involved in every decision that happens in my career" ("Twain Aiming").

How did Shania execute her decision to "divorce" Mary? Many country-music insiders speculate that a deal was cut. Some even go so far as to say (off the record) that Shania paid out a substantial amount of money. But no matter how it happened, the end result was that Mary Bailey did not continue to manage Shania into 1997.

In the end, Shania got what she felt she needed, but Mary had to relinquish the role that had brought her so much pleasure and excitement. To her everlasting credit, she has been consistently gracious about the whole affair, never hinting publicly that she feels anything but respect for Shania and her talent. When she does speak about the split, however, a note of sadness inevitably infuses her remarks:

I love her talent, I truly do, and I loved her like a child, like a daughter I never had. Because of my love I probably allowed things to happen that, strictly as business, I never would have accepted. I know this industry very well. I looked at her like an athlete going for the gold. When you see people who are that completely focused and determined, they sometimes fail to recognize that no one achieves their objectives alone. I understand that. It took a tremendous amount out of me emotionally. There are not enough words, it's beyond the call of duty what I did for her and her career and no one can take that away from me. It was not about money. I believed when no one else did and I mean no one. We had some very tough times. People ask me if it bothers me that she never mentions my name and I say no, not at all. I did not become involved for the glory. I did it because I felt the world had to see this exceptional talent. I truly loved her and I have nothing negative to say. She has now found happiness with Mutt, as well as overwhelming success, and through this, I hope will evolve the person I know is inside. (Leamer)

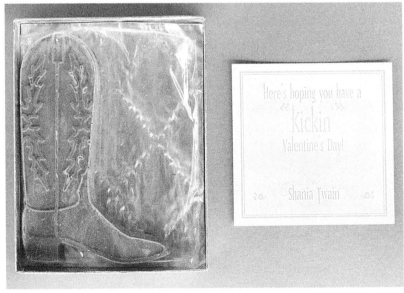

COURTESY BILL BORGWARDT

7

THE WOMAN IN ME (NEEDS THE MAN IN YOU)

Every June since 1990 — in fact, almost every June for the last twenty-five years — the Tennessee State Fair-grounds in Nashville become the center of the universe. At least it seems that way if you're a country-music fan or a worker for the cause. Twenty-four thousand fans shell out ninety dollars apiece to attend the Country Music Association/Grand Ole Opry co-sponsored Fan Fair, and every year the atmosphere is more electric than ever. Since 1990, tickets for the event have sold out months in advance. As Laurence Leamer writes, "Fan Fair [is] a feast of celebrity unlike anything else in American life. Movie stars sell access to the highest bidders, telling their tales in exchange for magazine cover stories and television coverage. Baseball players charge for their autographs. But country music is a moral universe of a far different standard. Almost all of the stars of country music come here . . . signing autographs for hours and singing on that great stage for no reward except the love of their fans."

For this one week in June, the Fan Fair site, a smattering of large, shedlike structures set around a stock-car racetrack, becomes a home away from home to enough people to populate a small city. As they roam the grounds, these people resolutely keep it light: they never jostle for position, they never even seem to get frustrated at the long lines or become cranky in the at times oppressive heat. These die-hard enthusiasts have assembled here to soak up the atmosphere, to tuck into some homestyle cuisine, and, above all, to mingle with the stars. Over one hundred of country's leading acts occupy visiting booths and play short sets in a never-ending succession on a stage erected in the center of the action.

If you called the Timmins branch of the Shania Twain Fan Club in the summer of 1997, you were treated to a long message about Shania's current schedule and plans. You were told that Shania was in the late stages of preparing a single, slated to be released in late July from her heavily anticipated follow-up to *The Woman in Me*. The new album, you were also informed, was consuming Shania night and day; she was striving to make it all come together by an unspecified date in the fall. Unfortunately, the message concluded, all of this meant that Shania would be unable to attend the 1997 Nashville Fan Fair. Judging by the tone of this announcement, you might deduce that Shania's scheduling conflict amounted to a national disaster. This is obviously absurd, but it does serve as a measure of just how important the Fan Fair had become since June of 1993 for both Shania and her fans.

For four straight years, Shania had made the most of the weeklong country celebration. Her decision not to attend the 1997 event, in career terms, was a risky one. By not being there, she was sacrificing a unique opportunity to reinvigorate her popularity for the sake of adhering to a tight production schedule, and only time will tell whether the gamble was worthwhile. There was

a personal aspect to all of this, as well. Forgoing the 1997
Fan Fair must have caused Shania some emotional strain.
The annual event was redolent with special memories for
her — it was a place she loved to be. Also, fair organizers
had made it known that only one year remained in their
lease on the original site. Shania will have just one more
chance, in 1998, to revisit the fair before the event is
moved to a slick new, downtown location and the humble,
rootsy intimacy of the original gathering is lost forever.

The Nashville Fan Fair has marked so many of the high
points of Shania's career. In 1995, for example, it became
the scene of *The Woman in Me's* triumph. That June, Shania
was unofficially crowned the Queen of Country: her
booth was one of the most heavily visited; her signature
was among the most frequently requested; and her three-
song set was the sensation of the week. One critic offers
his assessment of that performance: "Sashaying out on
stage, bottle of Canoe Springs held high, to the strains of
her breakthrough hit 'Whose Bed Have Your Boots Been
Under?,' Twain made major waves with the Fan Fair crowd
with her soulful singing, energetic presence and her
audience-wise stage patter" (Goldsmith).

When Shania, addressing the twenty thousand people
lining the grandstand, enquired "How's everybody doing?
How about you guys way up there?" the response was
deafening. Everybody — from fans, to industry insiders,
to media reps — was won over by her genuine warmth
and knock-out performance skills. After her set, she was
deluged with interview requests. Also during the 1995
festivities, Mercury surprised her with her first American
gold record and her first Canadian platinum disc. Then it
was Shania's turn to be blown away. Things don't get much
better than that. Fan Fair 1995, then, was when Shania
knew she had truly arrived: in the course of the week,

she entered the ranks of Garth, Clint, Reba, and Dolly. She became a bonafide country-music superstar.

By the time the 1996 Fan Fair kicked off, *The Woman in Me* was a platinum record in the U.S. as well. Many times over. Shania was the hottest female act in all of country music, and her album had even surpassed the sales records set by the late, great Patsy Cline. Leamer writes: "Shania was working Fan Fair with immense energy and savvy. . . . She was in her booth for two to four hours every day. Shania's people, unlike Reba's, counted the fans, making sure that everyone in line got an autograph." If, as Leamer claims, she occasionally seemed "like a mechanical doll, flashing a smile for their cameras, and then looking to the next person in line," it was quite simply because she had spent the previous eighteen months promoting *The Woman in Me* without respite, and here she was at Fan Fair 1996 giving everything she had left to give. Willingly. Happily. For the fans. She firmly believed she owed it to them. Naturally, there were moments when she had to retreat within herself just to retain her composure. The stress was unbelievable.

As the 1996 event progressed, Shania rallied and even shone. One evening, she met with a large group of disabled fans, and, continues Leamer, "She listened and talked to each of them. She came out from behind her booth and had time and emotion to spend with those who came to meet her. It was as if after months of hype and sales and image-making, she was confronted with a moment that touched her honestly and deeply. She talked to those fans as if something else was going on here today than creating an image that would sell seven million more CDs. . . . Shania talked to those disabled fans as if despite all her beauty and health and fame and wealth, she had some commonality with their lives, some touchstone with what they felt." Shania was and is a consummate professional, but she has never lost touch with her humanity. She has never forgotten, as she puts it, those "harsh lessons on the frailty of human life" she endured ("Fan Letter" 1994).

Shania has always displayed a willingness to reach out to those in need. When thirty-one-year-old Kentucky musician Bob Pruitt retired from performing because he was devastated by the death of his brother and band mate, Randy, Shania wrote to him, urging him to reconsider. "I know how devastating it can be to lose someone close to you," she said to her grieving colleague. "Sharing your musical talent doesn't mean you have to quit your job or make drastic changes. Life has a funny way of making our minds up for us. We've both learned the hard way" (Hitts). Shania cares as a way of life: her manifestation of interest in, and concern for, others is not merely a trick she likes to perform when all eyes are on her at the Nashville Fan Fair.

★ ★ ★

When Shania hit the Tennessee State Fairgrounds in June of 1993, there were no hordes of adoring fans waiting to meet her, no crush of reporters begging for interviews. She was lucky to have been invited at all. Many of the twenty-four thousand people in attendance would have had trouble identifying her. It was the last go-round for the hitless Shania Twain.

It was an inauspicious start to the week in which the best thing that ever happened to her would occur. Mutt Lange dropped by her booth, which that year was far from being a top draw. It couldn't have seemed like a momentous occasion at the time — just two telephone pals with a common interest in the music business finally meeting in person — but it was actually the beginning of a whole

BARB BLANCHARD/DAN PORTER, COURTESY *COUNTRY MUSIC NEWS*

new existence for Shania. Mutt, who hails from England, is an intensely private man (even somewhat reclusive). He is sixteen years older than Shania, and he's more at home in the rock world than the country world, but the two clicked. Shania loves to talk about Mutt, and to recall the early days of their relationship: "Mutt's a huge country music fan. I may be the princess in his life, but Tammy Wynette is the Queen!" She continues: "The steel guitar is his favorite instrument. He was a fan of mine through my first album and wanted to meet me. We first talked on the phone several weeks before we met in person. He got a hold of me through my manager. I had no idea he was a world famous record producer. I didn't read the back of pop and rock albums, which was good because I wasn't intimidated by him. Otherwise, I don't think I would have been able to express myself creatively without any inhibitions. It worked out really well. We became good friends over the phone, we were even writing songs and exchanging ideas. Creatively we were very in sync with each other. The first time I actually talked to him face to face was in Nashville during Mercury's Fan Fair show in '93, and we haven't wanted to be apart from that moment on" (Geocites).

Initially, their union was platonic: most of the time they spent together was devoted to Shania's music. They explored the possibility of working together on the follow-up to *Shania Twain*, but because they were both so frantically busy, finding the requisite block of time proved extremely difficult. Shania was still promoting her first album, and Mutt was in heavy demand — the records he had produced for a range of rock artists had collectively sold more than one hundred million copies. So he and Shania continued to work over the phone whenever they could, and they met whenever their schedules could be made to mesh. Love blossomed between them on a working trip to Europe. Shania pinpoints the moment it occurred: it was in romantic, sunny Spain. And, as is often the way with these things, it just seemed to come out of the blue. "Looking at him the day I fell in love, and looking at him the day before?" Shania remarks: "Two different things" (Schneller).

Equipped with a 2.5-carat diamond ring, Mutt popped the question when the pair arrived in Paris. Shania had fallen hard. She accepted immediately. Mutt flew Jill and Carrie-Ann over to keep her company and share in the excitement while he tied up the loose ends of a recording commitment. Finally, just over six months after they met at the Nashville Fan Fair, Shania and Mutt returned to North America to be married. On 28 December 1993, they were wed on Shania's home turf: Huntsville. It was a magical, joyous occasion. Surrounded by her sisters and the entire Twain family, Shania celebrated. A miraculous year — which had seen her rise from drudgery and obscurity to undreamed-of heights — was drawing to a close, and a bright new future was dawning.

As 1994 got under way, Shania and Mutt adjusted to their new life together, establishing domestic and working routines. They began to write the material that would comprise *The Woman in Me*. Though they share writing credits on ten of the album's twelve songs, most of the tracks were based on ideas that Shania says she "was writing before I even met Mutt" (Brown). Still, Mutt's influence was incalculable. His track record proves that he had the necessary skills — Mutt is an accomplished, Grammy-award-winning songwriter in his own right.

Shania explains: "A lot of those ideas were things I was working on before I met him, but when you get together with the right person, all the right things seem to start happening. He comes from the rock world, so he's got so much spunk to his music. But obviously, we have a much closer relationship than your average co-writers. We sit around and write songs during commercial breaks while we're watching TV, or while we're going for groceries. It's almost like extended conversation for us. If there's nothing to talk about, we make something up, and that's what songwriting's all about" (Powell). From this seamless, easygoing partnership were spun the songs that were destined to carry Shania over the top. It gives a whole new meaning to the expression "labor of love." And egos remained unbruised. "If anything it's fun," Shania says of writing with Mutt. "We're not artsy people. We're everyday people who like to throw around creative ideas" ("Shania Twain's Musical Marriage").

Then there was the question of Mutt's technical wizardry. The role it played in the success of *The Woman in Me* cannot be overestimated. Luke Lewis, in fact, says: "You can't take away [Mutt's technical] contribution to the record. I don't mean to be mean, but you could play this record with no vocals and it would be an entertaining and interesting record" (Leamer). And neither can the importance of Mutt's money and power within the industry — which derived from that technical skill — be exaggerated. Later, as he worked over Shania's music in the recording studio, he insisted that it meet the same technical standards that he had set for the work of such front-runners as AC/DC, Bryan Adams, and Michael Bolton. Shania, Mutt felt, was in the same league. And that would mean he'd need the same resources — the kind of money a Nashville record label would be loathe to put up.

In the end, it took more than half a million dollars to make *The Woman in Me*. The figure shocked Music City:

it was almost five times what a typical American country album costs. When Mercury balked at dispensing that much cash for a follow-up to a less than successful, hitless album, Mutt and Mercury president Luke Lewis struck a deal. Mutt was a millionaire. His faith in both his own abilities and those of his new wife had prompted him to put his money where his mouth is. He would shoulder the bulk of the financial responsibility for making Shania's new album. That way, both he and Shania knew, the record they made would sound exactly the way they wanted it to sound — in other words, the way it *should* sound. Mutt, then, was not only Shania's producer: he was also a shareholder in her future and Mercury Nashville's full business partner. "Mutt bore the risks as much as we did," Lewis says. "That's a beautiful relationship to have with a creative producer" (Leamer).

With Mercury's risk minimized, Mutt was unfettered. He entered the studio with Shania; she was now a calm professional who'd been there before and knew the ropes. This time, however, there were two enormous differences: she was backed to the hilt by a producer who had absolute faith in her as an artist, and she was recording her own material. The freedom was wonderful, but no one was deluded enough to believe that there wasn't a great deal at stake. Shania was putting herself on the line. Looking back, she reflects on how far off the mark their expectations turned out to be: "We never really expected [this success early on]," she says. "We were excited about it. I was excited as a songwriter, because I was finally getting a chance to record my own music. I remember at the time thinking, 'Wouldn't this be exciting if this went platinum?' Then when it went platinum I thought, 'Oh boy, certainly three would just be totally unbelievable.' Then, of course, when it got past that. . . . You never really think at the time of breaking records" (Cohen).

Her husband's belief in her continued to revitalize her belief in herself, and this dynamic pushed Shania to deliver an unparalleled performance. She never felt she was receiving special treatment from Mutt, though. Mutt demanded the best and brought out the best in everyone he worked with. "He enhances the artist's music," Shania maintains. "A lot of the success of [*The Woman in Me*] has to do with the writing and what he has done with the sound of it. Right from the beginning he said, 'We need to go into your catalogue. I want to know what you've been writing, then we'll go from there. You be the basis to the creativity of this album, because it needs to be you, not me. . . .' And so, that's what we did" (Brown). There was an abundance of creativity all round. *The Woman in Me* doesn't sound like any country album that preceded it. Though plenty of people urged Mutt and Shania not to stray too far from the tried and true, as a team they broached virgin territory and never gave in to the pressure to conform: "I think there were times when the label was a little nervous, a little cautious," Shania says, "but we stuck to our plan" (Richmond).

The Woman in Me may still be the most expensive country recording ever made. It took a year to produce. Mutt had such a keen sense of what contemporary audiences were looking for that every track was a mini-epic of master production. Each song was constructed of layer upon layer of sound: little hooks and flourishes were woven into an unprecedented sonic tapestry. The project migrated from studio to studio, beginning at the Sound Stage in Nashville where Mutt lay down the basic instrumental tracks with engineer Ron "Snake" Williams, and then moving through three other Nashville locations where overdubs were done under the auspices of three more engineers. Finally, the entire package was mixed in Quebec, Canada.

It was an arduous process, but well worth it. Just listen to the results. The finished product is an intriguing melange: a little rock, a little pop, a dash of R&B, and a healthy dose of pedal steel. There is a distinctively Cajun feel to the work, as well. "A lot of the album has a bit of Cajun Flavor, Cajun fiddle," Shania acknowledges. "I think the whole idea behind the fiddle on this CD is that we wanted fiddle that really 'dug in,' and it was really aggressive, not just the fiddle as a background instrument" (Brown). "If Mutt Lange had been a chef," Leamer notes, "his restaurant would have featured an international cuisine that tasted a bit like southern cooking, a touch of French, something Italian, and Chinese and Japanese too — a smidgen of everything for the price of one meal." Their chemistry bubbling, Mutt and Shania had whipped up something fresh-tasting and thoroughly delectable.

To all the musicians who helped them to achieve this brave new sound, Shania and Mutt owed a debt of gratitude. In her liner notes for *The Woman in Me*, Shania wrote: "Thanks to all the Nashville musicians who worked so long and hard to get it all just right. You guys are really the best there is." They had to be: Mutt was absolutely uncompromising.

Virtually everyone agreed. *The Woman in Me* was in an entirely different league than *Shania Twain*. If you listened to the albums back-to-back, you might even have thought that you were listening to two individual artists. A few of *Woman*'s reviews were mixed. Some of the writers just didn't seem to know what to make of the record. It sounded great, most of them conceded, but was it country? A reviewer for Canada's *Country* magazine encapsulated what the album had going for it and what it was up against:

On the surface, there isn't much about Shania Twain in *The Woman in Me* that rings true. Women who meet and marry big-name producers and subsequently release sumptuously produced big-label albums can expect to be greeted with as many smirks as smiles. Oh, and she's drop-dead gorgeous in that country-marketable way as well, which should bring the claws out in all quarters.

Credit rock heavyweight Mutt Lange with seeing something in his future wife besides the farm-girl fantasy beauty. In an MOR-clogged "New Country" industry, Twain has enough of the real and the unreal to live up to her label. . . . A record with this kind of gloss will be greeted with open arms in some quarters (radio), suspicion in others. . . . Lange's production doesn't hurt either. Rock-conscious enough for the sound to jump when it has to, country-savvy enough for the pedal steels and harps to hit their marks, Lange knows what works. (Lepage)

But Mutt and Shania understood the industry well enough to expect a bit of a backlash. They weathered the initial storm proudly; their belief in the album and each other was stronger than anything the critics could dish out. Ultimately, they knew, it was the fans who would decide whether *The Woman in Me* was a viable product.

When it became apparent that those fans were preparing to slap their massive seal of approval on the disc, the critical rhetoric quickly changed. In fact, a whole new language began to evolve as country-music journalists struggled to find ways of describing what Shania and Mutt had created. Pretty soon, Shania was being called a "country-rock" star — the emphasis falling heavily, of course, on "country." Even the *New York Times* attempted to get a handle on things by resorting to a laundry list of comparisons: "Several rock styles appear on *The Woman in Me*, from poppy riffs that sound borrowed from Buddy Holly's song book to a thumping back beat reminiscent of Queen. Yet Ms. Twain's arrangements are dominated by country standbys like pedal steel guitar, fiddle and mandolin, and her songs are in the mould of those traditional country superstars like George Jones and Tammy Wynette" (Stovall).

Such reviews inadvertently boosted Shania onto an exciting new echelon. By mentioning her in the same breath as some of the world's most famous rock and country artists, they were implying that she belonged in such lofty company. She was gaining acceptance fast and being pegged as an innovator. The *Times* added: "Perhaps rock's influence on Ms. Twain is not so much musical as it is philosophical. Rock's iconoclasm has freed her from country's tradition and allowed her to create a country music that is hers alone" (Stovall).

Shania did the interview thing to promote her groundbreaking new album, and as she went along, more details of her dynamic collaboration with Mutt came to light. Mutt had pushed Shania harder and further as an artist than anyone else had done before. During the songwriting process, especially, he had challenged her to cast off the constraining conventions and structures of country and exploit a wide range of ideas and styles. "He's made me a much better writer," she declared. "He sends me away and says, 'No, that lyric's not quite there yet.'" To illustrate her point, Shania talked about "Any Man of Mine," explaining that the song was originally called "This Man of Mine." "It was all about how great and wonderful this guy was," she says. "But Mutt came up with a new guitar riff that changed the whole tone. We rewrote it and the lyrics became spunkier and, really, more like me" (Jennings). Out of such experimentation a more forthright musical persona was born — Shania Twain as butt-kicking "macho female." In this sense, she was now a little like Courtney Love or Alanis Morissette, but the resemblance obviously ended there.

The spunk appealed to the fans. So did virtually everything else about the album and the videos that were released to support it. Country video programmers felt the heat; initially reluctant to run the first of these clips — "Whose Bed Have Your Boots Been Under?" — they soon bowed to popular demand. One of the most overtly traditional country tracks on the record, the song was released first to pave the way for the album's more un-orthodox material. "Any Man of Mine" was issued as a single and video soon afterwards, and then the album really started to move off record-store shelves. Requests

BARB BLANCHARD/DAN PORTER, COURTESY *COUNTRY MUSIC NEWS*

for the two singles poured in to radio and television stations. Both rose steadily up the charts.

Five months later, as the 1995 Fan Fair got under way, *The Woman in Me* had gone gold; it was number four with a bullet on the *Billboard* country charts. It had, in this short span of time, already massively outsold *Shania Twain*, and it looked as though its ascent up the charts would continue. Yet a number of Nashville insiders still considered its success a fluke. Around the Fan Fair that year, there was some talk that the album would crash and burn. Famous last words. After the Mercury showcase performances, a throng of producers, managers, songwriters, and performers fought for backstage passes. They were dying to meet the label's latest phenomenon.

Despite such clear indicators of success, Shania, Mutt, and their team could not just sit back and ride the wave. They had to sell the album while it was hot with all the energy and ingenuity they could muster. A bold new album demanded a bold new marketing strategy. There would be no Triple Play-style antics this time: *The Woman in Me* was going to sink or swim on its own. The promotional campaign that Mercury, Mutt, and Shania devised and orchestrated centered on Shania's Cinderella life story and her exceptional physical assets. They enlisted Hollywood's own John and Bo Derek to assist with all the visual promo material — everything from still photos and album art to those first two videos. Shania's image was completely recast.

The metamorphosis was stunning. There would be no more shots of Shania bundled in parkas. What was the point when the sight of her in crop-tops and skin-tight hip-hugger pants was enough to bring on heart palpitations in most male observers? Her new, high-powered marketing machine pumped out an array of goodies: a

Shania Twain calendar, shot by Bo and John, which was
sent to radio programmers; a chocolate boot and a Shania
card, which were issued for Valentine's day; and life-size
cutouts of Shania, in high-heeled boots with her mid-
riff exposed, which were shipped to record stores. The
marketing of *The Woman in Me* revolutionized the way
country music was sold. The days of rhinestones, big hair,
and intimate live performances were over: country had
entered the age of spandex and the erotically charged
video.

Shania drew a lot of flak. She was rocking the boat with
her crossover sound, her aggressively manufactured sexy
image, her noisy sales push — and a lot of industry people
didn't appreciate it. Some suggested that her album was
selling on the basis of her looks alone. Shania calmly
dismissed such accusations: "The success started with the
music, and it will continue with the music. No one's going
to care what Shania Twain looks like in '97 if the [next]
album isn't great" (Powell). At the same time, no one
involved with *The Woman in Me* had any illusions: Shania's
looks were a great marketing advantage, one they would
be fools not to exploit. With a measure of restraint. "It
is a cheesecake image," one *Billboard* correspondent explained, "but not a cheesy cheesecake image. She's
nobody's Barbie doll" ("Gold Country"). And, in her own
way, Shania also makes it clear that she, too, grasps the
implications of the way *The Woman in Me* and her image
have been promoted: "Someone said to me once, 'Well,
if I had your belly-button I'd sell 8 million albums too.'
But it takes a lot more than a belly-button to sell more
than 8 million albums" ("Gold Country").

Big record label, crack promotion team, Svengali-like
husband aside, Shania is her own woman. If she hadn't
wholeheartedly endorsed the image makeover, it wouldn't

have happened. If she hadn't already exuded a certain natural sexiness, she wouldn't have allowed it to be superimposed upon her — a film of makeup, hairspray, and revealing costumes. She believes that those who chastize her for showing off her belly button need to reevaluate their own sexual politics. They need to think about the way *they* objectify women. Their reaction to her, she says, "goes to show me that we still have a ways to go as women. I don't mind proving myself, but I refuse to play down my looks. I'm not going to have this figure when I'm 50 — I want to enjoy it now. Why should I have to downplay the way I look so that people take my artistry more seriously?" (Chodan, "La Belle Shania"). In the final analysis, the only critics who matter to Shania are her fans, and they've communicated to her, time and time again, that both her image and her music are just fine by them.

The videos, those potent cocktails of image and music, captivated those fans. John and Bo Derek directed the "Whose Bed Have Your Boots Been Under?" clip. It was the first out of the gate. In it, Shania, clad in a sexy red dress, dances seductively on a diner countertop and flirts with dozens of oblivious "average Joes." Jaws dropped all over Nashville whenever it came on. What manner of country video was this? Only the fact that Shania was so playful, that she was obviously enjoying the lark, kept things from getting out of hand. But when the initial shock wore off, everyone realized that Shania was actually singing a standout, up-tempo country song. Its saucy lyrics were both tough and funny, and its choral hook was nothing short of infectious. "Whose Bed," ultimately, was the perfect first single: for male fans, it provided plenty of eye candy; for the women, it became a "don't put up with his crap" anthem. And everyone could appreciate

John Hughey's rock-solid pedal-steel work, Joe Spivey's blistering fiddle, and the bizarrely appropriate do-wop background vocals. It was a dynamite package.

The album's second video and single, "Any Man of Mine," picked up right where its predecessor left off. Its opening fiddle line is a powerful attack — it works like a lead-guitar riff in a heavy-rock song, setting up the anthemic quality of the tune. From the first notes, you could tell the song was destined to become a classic. It has a much stronger rock sensibility, however, than "Whose Bed," so much so that it pushed the goodwill of some country fans to the limit. But while the drum line for "Any Man" owes more to heavy metal than to the Grand Ole Opry, the song still *feels* country. Similarly, the playful woman in the John Derek-produced video, cavorting with dogs and a horse on an idyllic ranch, is at once a fresh-faced, hardworking farm girl and a sexy siren sporting a crop-top and cowboy hat. The tune is catchy, the lyrics are smart and funny, the performer is self-assured. Country and rock meet in this clip and blend harmoniously and memorably. In a press release accompanying *The Woman in Me*, Shania comments: "I think ['Any Man of Mine'] could be the impact song on the album. It is an excellent combination of the two of us [Shania and Mutt]. It's got everything that he's known for as a producer and a writer, yet it's so me it's not funny." The lady was right: "Any Man" did become the "impact song." Its success alone could have made the album a monster hit.

The third release represented a change of pace: the melancholy, country-pop title ballad. "The Woman in Me (Needs the Man in You)" is an emotional tour de force that established Shania as a brilliant vocal talent. The video of this song was the most exotic, and arguably the most sensual, of them all, thanks to director Markus

Blunder, a gorgeous desert setting (complete with majestic pyramids), and Shania's performance. She dances alone in a diaphanous white dress; the purity and innocence she radiates are spiced with a smoky sexuality. Here the veneer of toughness that makes both "Whose Bed" and "Any Man of Mine" seem so attitude-driven finally cracks. In "Woman," Shania articulates — with both lyrics and images — her vulnerability, fallibility, and need. The long, soaring notes of the chorus are heartbreaking.

The next four singles released from *The Woman in Me* were accompanied by lush state-of-the-art videos directed by Steve Goldmann. "(If You're Not in It for Love) I'm Outta Here!," "You Win My Love," and "No One Needs to Know" kicked things back into high gear, while "Home Ain't Where His Heart Is (Anymore)," a timeless country ballad, proved that "The Woman in Me" single was no one-shot deal. It was becoming clear that *The Woman in Me* album was a hit factory.

Dressed in her Shania Twain costume — form-fitting, low-rise pants and tight, cropped red sweater — Mercury's newest hot commodity romps through the "Outta Here" clip with a throng of young men and women who bear no resemblance to the stereotypical country fan. This song, this video, scream "Crossover!" The slide guitar in "Outta Here" glides through a rock riff right out of Def Leppard. It's a musical celebration, and everyone is invited — honky-tonk folks and club kids alike. "You Win My Love," the only song on the album penned by Mutt alone, is also an irresistible pop-rock hit, and it strays further from country than anything else on *The Woman in Me*. In the video, Shania's done up like a race-car-driving supermodel, right down to the Cindy Crawford beauty mark, and she's obviously having a blast driving a supercharged go-cart.

For the "No One Needs to Know" clip, Goldmann intercut raw footage of tornadoes with jam-session sequences, thereby signaling the song's inclusion on the soundtrack of the blockbuster film *Twister* (another coup for Shania and Mutt). The more interesting aspect of this video is its live-performance opening segment. Shania, with a band behind her, counts in, plays, and sings the opening strains of the up-tempo, rockabilly-flavored acoustic number. It could be that Shania did this to thumb her nose at her detractors — those who were trying to cut her down to size by saying that she was incapable of reproducing the album live.

The fourth and final Goldmann video was for *The Woman in Me*'s seventh single: "Home Ain't Where His Heart Is (Anymore)." Shania had written the song a couple of years before the release of the album. Its chorus was the first thing that Shania ever sang to Mutt — she did it during one of their early phone conversations. "That's when he realized I had writing potential he wanted to tap into," she says. "It's the first song we ended up completing together, the first song we demoed, the first one we recorded in the studio in Nashville, and the first song we mixed and completed" (Press Release). "Home" is a real hurtin' song — an emotionally charged ballad about change. Its subtle black-and-white companion video, with its occasional bursts of color, is a moving reflection of the desolate sadness the song probes.

"God Bless the Child" is, in Shania's words, "a lullaby I wrote after my parents died. I would go for long walks in the bush by myself with this song swimming around in my head. I really didn't know where the melody came from. When I met Mutt, I sang it for him and he said 'Wow — that's beautiful!' We didn't even change it. There's no chorus, no verse, just a thought . . . no story, no hook, nothing commercial at all about it. It's just a true sincere thought and emotion" (Press Release). The album track is a haunting a cappella wail — unadulterated and gut-wrenching. It's a prayer. An addendum to *The Woman in Me*'s more radio-friendly offerings. Certainly not an obvious choice for the album's final single.

Late in 1996, however, Shania and Mutt decided to go back into the studio and recut the song. They orchestrated it and fleshed it out with new lyrics. Pop-soul band Take 6 was brought in to help achieve an even fuller gospel feel. The single was released over the holiday season as a kind of seasonal gift to Shania's fans. The video for the new and improved "God Bless the Child" was directed by Larry Jordan and features not only Shania and members of Take 6 but also a children's choir. In a warehouse setting, Shania belts out her emotional plea wearing simple, modest clothing. For the first time, her sexually provocative image is nowhere in evidence. The message here is about caring for the world's underprivileged children — there is no room for flirtatiousness or posturing of any kind.

The Woman in Me also features four other tracks. On a weaker album, they could all have been potential singles. "Is There Life after Love?" and "Raining on Our Love" are both pretty ballads, though neither really soars like the title track or "Home Ain't Where His Heart Is." The laid-back country-rocker "If It Don't Take Two," however, is a "me and my baby" number that could quite easily have become a popular hit. And "Leaving Is the Only Way Out" is one hell of a hurtin' song that does Shania's country roots proud. But, whatever their merits, these tunes would not venture out into the marketplace solo. Shania and her support structure had begun to worry about the overkill factor: no matter how Shania-crazy the record-buying public had become, Nashville's newest hit-maker, whatever she did, had to avoid oversaturating the country market. There is a lot of wisdom in the old cliché, "Leave 'em wanting more."

Shania did stop just short of oversaturation, and her restraint paid off. They did want more — and more. Despite the fact that she wasn't touring her breakthrough album, she was in great demand. Throughout 1995 and 1996, her schedule was so hectic that she and Mutt had little time to themselves. Their marriage was still relatively new, and this near-total absence of privacy and leisure was difficult to bear at times. *The Woman in Me*, Shania admitted, "has done so well for me, it's had such a long life, that it's worn me out in a way" (Muretich). The album's success also gave rise to a brand-new set of pressures. Suddenly, Shania was both a sex symbol mooned over by lovestruck male fans and the object of media scrutiny. No longer the tireless self-promoter, she was now a member of the celebrity elite, which the media actively seek out. Reporters scrambled for her opinions on anything and everything. Almost overnight, what Shania ate, wore, did, and said became newsworthy. She was learning what life in a fishbowl is all about.

Things look very different through that glass partition. Being on the receiving end of all that attention has given Shania a unique perspective on the trials and tribulations of being a beautiful female entertainer. "Groupies," for example, in her experience, behave differently towards women. "I think guys can be just as enamoured of success as girls but they're a little more shy about expressing it," she notes. "So it's my female fans that cry or get excited. The guys, well they just kind of freeze up" (Muretich).

Still, Shania also believes that the general response to her attitude-laden lyrics — like the reaction to those of

Alanis Morissette — indicates that men are coming to terms with the idea of the powerful female: "I just sense that in a lot of things — in books that I'm reading or movies that I watch. . . . Men just seem to be more responsive to women's needs and women seem to be more responsive to men's needs. . . . And that's kind of what I'm having fun with in my songs. It's not a rebellious or negative point of view. It's really just saying, 'Look, we know nobody's perfect.' Whether you're a guy or a girl, here's a few lyrics to make you laugh at yourself a little bit. That's really what a song like 'Any Man of Mine' is about" (Howell).

A story one fan told her about the effect the smash hit had on her life illustrates her point. The woman, Shania says, was barbecuing a steak for her husband when the phone rang. She rushed off to answer it, leaving the meat on the grill. "When she came back out to the barbecue," reports Shania, "everything was burned black. And she saw her husband standing there, and she thought he was just going to kill her. But he just said, 'Mmmm, I like it like that,' picking up the line from the song, and she was just in tears. It was really sweet that he responded like that. It just goes to show you this song is not . . . rebellious, it's not that far off reality. Men are so much more like that these days. Women and men are becoming more compatible I think" (Howell).

Shania's sense of the current state of sexual politics is filtered through her relationship with Mutt. And their compatibility is a product of their respect for each other's differences — career and personal. Shania's success, this monolith that they forged together, now keeps them apart for long stretches of time; under these circumstances, a marriage has to have a strong foundation — mutual respect — if it is to survive. As the promotional blitz for

The Woman in Me began to wind down, Shania started to think about how soon she could begin work on her third album. Her strong creative drive was certainly behind this impulse, but another important motivator was the fact that it would mean she could see a lot more of her husband. Mutt, she says, is "a very humble guy and basically doesn't want to be a star. He just wants to be a person who makes the music." Because of his retiring nature, Shania had to spend almost two years promoting her record without him: "He never comes with me . . . I don't think he ever will, and I totally understand where he comes from" ("Shania's Alone"). Robert John "Mutt" Lange is an enigmatic individual who has rarely even been photographed. He is secretive about his private life because he wants to keep it that way: private.

Mutt does, however, respect Shania's stardom, and doesn't begrudge her the time he knows she has to give to her career and the fans who allow it to exist. And, in turn, Shania defers to Mutt's desire for anonymity. Mutt "doesn't want to be a star," she's often said; he made that clear early in their relationship (Keyes). Shania scrupulously avoids talking to journalists about their private life. She has, however, frequently acknowledged the huge role he's played in her rise to stardom, and identifies him as the major source of her personal happiness. Because, even though Shania may appear to be doing things her way, she knows she could never do them alone: the woman in her, clearly, needs the man in Mutt. "I sang ['God Bless the Child'] until I met Mutt," she confides. "I felt totally lost, and that song was my crying out . . . I don't feel lost anymore" (Lague).

8

IN IT
FOR LOVE

Shania's third wedding anniversary came and went, and 1996 receded into history. *The Woman in Me* was now an artifact, a classic. Everyone seemed to have a copy, and so the sales push ended. The album had generated no fewer than five number-one hits and garnered over twenty major awards. Shania had attended most of the awards ceremonies and had performed at many of them before auditoriums filled with members of the industry's elite, dressed in their best and proud to be honoring country's biggest stars.

Throughout 1995 and 1996, Shania had collected trophies and plaques from the Canadian Country Music Association, as well as from SOCAN and the Country Radio Broadcasters. She had received an American Music Award, a Grammy, a few Junos, a couple of Academy of Country Music Awards and Golden Picks, prizes from RPM and Blockbuster, and a World Music Award. Not a bad haul. As she headed into the fall of 1996, just about the only honor she hadn't yet won was the prestigious Country Music Association crystal trophy.

The winners of this prize were chosen in Nashville by the voting members of the CMA, the core of the country-music industry. Shania was nominated in three categories. In her mind, a CMA award ranked among country's top prizes, and she longed to have one. "I have to admit that being accepted by the industry you work amongst and with means a lot," she said ("Twain Aiming"). Mercury and her management wanted the prize so badly for her that they erected a Shania billboard on Nashville's Music Row and started a postcard campaign, targeting CMA voters and extolling the star's achievements. One CMA member called it "the most aggressive campaign I've ever seen coming out of Nashville" ("Twain Best New Artist"). The awards ceremony was held the evening of 2 October 1996. As the festivities drew to a close, Shania left for home empty-handed.

Many feel, though, that Shania's big night at the CMA Awards is still to come. Charlie Chase and Lorianne Crook, cohosts of an influential country-music talk show, believe that Shania's enormous popular appeal was her undoing in 1996. "Shania is going through a little bit of what Billy Ray Cyrus went through, hitting so fast and so big," Crook argues. "The industry doesn't tend to show respect with their votes to that kind of success." Chase agrees, and predicts: "That respect will come. The industry just doesn't know her as well as the fans do" (Hayden). Shania took the disappointment in stride. She had to maintain her perspective. After all, *The Woman in Me* had been a monumental success in virtually every other regard.

As 1997 dawned, Shania suddenly found herself in the by now unfamiliar position of being able to relax a little — to marshall her energies and to reflect on her future. Upstate New York beckoned. Shania and Mutt could now spend some time together enjoying their ranch, their stables, and the new house they'd built in a hybrid style

Shania describes as "Mediterranean-meets-Adirondacks" (Lague). Maybe the two of them could start writing some new material and eventually head into the recording studio they were constructing on their property. More than anything, though, Shania was looking forward to slipping into some comfortable clothes and relishing a moment of freedom from the public eye. Here, at home, she could just be herself — a young woman in love. She could even unpack. "Three weeks out of every month I'm gone for meetings and promotion work, and I'm only home two or three days at a time," she explained, speaking of her rollercoaster ride of the previous year. "I usually have three suitcases full. I don't even unpack, I just switch things in and out" (Beck). In 1997, Shania could shove those empty suitcases under the bed for awhile.

Does this ranch idyll with Mutt seem just too perfect, too well deserved, to be true? Well it was and it wasn't. Shania was granted this welcome respite, but all the while her peace of mind was marred by family problems. And when you're a celebrity, family problems often equal ugly scandal. What's yours is ours, is the motto of the tabloid press. Because of their sister's fame, when Mark and Darryl Twain — now both in their early twenties — were arrested in May of 1996 for attempting to break into a Huntsville car dealership (Mark was also charged with mischief and assaulting a police officer), it was major news.

Shania had been worrying about her brothers for a long time. They walked on the wild side, and she'd struggled to control them when they were in her care during the Huntsville years. But she believed in them, and prayed that as her star ascended, they'd get their own lives on track. It wasn't to be. While she was in Timmins for the Shania Twain Day festivities, Mark was just beginning to serve a six-month sentence. By February of 1997, Darryl had joined his brother in jail. In sentencing Mark, Judge Douglas Bice noted that having a famous relative could be problematic for some people, and it seems he was right (Hickey). When Shania's older sister, Jill, was arrested for setting fire to an ex-boyfriend's property shortly thereafter, Bice's words appeared downright prophetic. Yet Mark, Darryl, and Jill are all adults who've made their own choices. They are accountable for their own actions. It's unfair to both Shania and the Twain family to use these troubles as a means of calling Shania's character into question.

Just to add insult to injury, in the fall of 1996 the wire services picked up on this "scandalous" tidbit: a probe had been instigated to determine whether the recording studio Shania and Mutt were building on their Adirondack property was in violation of local zoning regulations. Headlines like "Shania in Trouble with Law" cropped up in some newspapers. A mountain was clearly being made out of a molehill. Shania and Mutt could only shake their heads and get on with it.

Shania had to clear her mind. The blaring scandal-sheet headlines, the buzz of malicious speculation, threatened her happiness, her personal equilibrium. So she filled her head with music. She popped *The Woman in Me* into the CD player and finally listened to it in peace, with a little objective distance. She knew it was a good record. A great one even. She'd established some pretty high standards for herself. Now, at last, Shania also had the chance to explore what everybody else in the country had been doing in the past year. To her amazement, she began to realize that, in many cases, she and Mutt had set the standard. *New Country* magazine's "The Year's Best" issue endorsed this notion. Its cover story indicated that *The*

Woman in Me had sent shockwaves through Music City. Single-handedly, it argued, Shania had changed the face of country:

> In time, country music's largest audience turned into proud cravers of Shania. . . . And Nashville tried to provide more of the vibe — not Shania wanna-bes, exactly, of which there were an expected obvious few, but debut male and female artists alike who expressed Twain's underlying message that an ordinary person with artistry and a touch or two of star quality could make the kind of genuine although not roots-obsessed music for which [Garth] Brooks paved the way. Albums by [these] newcomers . . . were all quite different. But they shared things. . . . They were People Like Shania, and they often sounded that way as well, choosing whatever they liked from rock and pop to arrive at an encouraging amount of unfettered new country. (Hunter)

But, of course, nobody could do it better than Shania — with the able assistance of Mutt. Other forms of homage, other symbols of the cultural impact Shania had made with *The Woman in Me*, were springing up all over: country funnyman Cledus T. Judd, for example, recorded a "tribute single" entitled "If Shania Was Mine," Canadian vocalist Donna Huber and a backup band took Shania's music on tour, Huber billing herself as "Shania Twin." There was even a stripper who shopped her wares throughout Quebec and Ontario using the stage name "Shania Twins." Imitation, as they say, is the sincerest form of flattery.

The Woman in Me's infiltration of record collections the world over also created two other new realities: expectations for Shania's next project would be sky high, and she would be able to enjoy absolute artistic autonomy without backing her next undertaking with Twain-Lange money. By the fall of 1996, the ideas behind *Come on Over* were already gaining momentum. Shania was undaunted: "If anything, this album is going to come together a lot easier since we're now accepted as a team. In the beginning, we had to prove ourselves. So there was a lot more stress there. We were experimenting with something that was new for country, a new sound, a new attitude. Now, everybody's doing it. That's given us the ticket to set the precedent once again — and this time people won't be as reluctant to accept it" (Muretich).

Can Shania duplicate her previous success? Better than anyone, she knows that this is in many ways beyond her control. "You can't anticipate that sort of thing," she remarks sagely. "All I can say is that I'm giving more of myself for this album, so I'm hoping for better results" (Krewen, "There's a Better Album"). She also knows she's got some goods to deliver. "I've got years of ideas," she says. "I've been writing since I was a very young girl. I'm not ready to run out of ideas yet" ("Shania at Ease").

In fact, she's even willing to go out on a limb and promise a deeper, more heartfelt record, one that takes "another step." "It doesn't mean drastic change," she says, "it just means different — different enough to still lead as opposed to follow" ("Twain Promises"). Elsewhere she elaborates: "There's definitely going to be some grooves and some feels on this album that you didn't get on *The Woman in Me* and at the same time you're going to get some of the same stuff. I'm not drifting that far away from who I am. *The Woman in Me* truly was a very good reflection of me. The new album will be definitely that, and more" (Krewen, "There's a Better Album").

Shania is adamant that she will not be serving reheated leftovers when she ventures forth to sell *Come on Over*.

"We don't want to make another *The Woman in Me*. There will be similarities but we're also trying out new ideas. I don't want to stay in the same place musically. I want to keep moving all the time. Right now, that's more important than anything" (Richmond). With statements such as these, Shania betrays her ambition — but this only means that she wants to be as good as she can be. Stagnation is anathema to her. She was born to be on the move. Shania is not ruthlessly ambitious. Neither does she really want to be "bigger than country," as some have suggested ("Gold Country"). She will remain, first and foremost, a country entertainer, but that won't prevent her from trying her hand at other things.

Acting? Maybe. "I get a lot of scripts," she reveals, "but I can quickly reduce the number that might interest me. . . . Besides, it's never really been my goal to become an actress. . . . If I ever do chose to do a movie I'd want to make sure I was good at it. So, it might be a while before I take anybody up on a film offer. . . . I've got too much to do anyway" (Muretich). So Shania may well follow her girlhood idol Dolly Parton into the film world, but not before she's convinced herself that she, like Dolly, has got what it takes to do it right.

For the time being, Shania is completely absorbed in her next recording project. She's even been declining personal appearances and interviews; they are just too distracting. By April of 1997, she was doing nothing else. To the suggestion that she'd dropped out of sight because she was experiencing a lapse in productivity — just resting — she replied with mock indignation: "Time off? How dare you! I haven't taken any time off at all. We were writing songs sporadically here and there over the last two years, but then the time came when I said 'OK, that's it. I'm no longer promoting *The Woman in Me*.' There has to be an end to the promotion and performances and appearances. So I went into songwriting gear. That's what I've been doing! We've got 16 songs that we're working on for this album. That's a lot of material" (Krewen, "There's a Better Album"). Fans got a taste of what to expect on the new album when the single "Love Gets Me Every Time" began making the rounds of radio stations in late September.

And when *Come on Over* is out, Shania says, all those rumors about her not being able to perform live will be quashed once and for all. She's going on tour. "Right now we're right in the middle of making the album and we just can't pinpoint when we'll finish," she explained. "But we plan on following the release of the album very shortly with a tour, so hopefully that'll be sometime in early 1998. I'm very anxious to get out there and do my thing. . . . I've done a few key television performances, but there's all the more need for me to get out there and really do it" (Krewen, "There's a Better Album").

One evening a few years back, Shania was the guest of honor at a Nashville party. She had just received her first platinum record, and the cream of Music City had been invited to celebrate the occasion. The champagne flowed. Boisterous congratulations were delivered. A couple of days later, Shania watched herself go through it all again on television. Only then, observers report, did she realize that she had "enjoyed that night" (Leamer). It was as if she were watching it all happen to someone else. In retrospect, Shania has said that she was too "focused" on the astonishing events that were transforming her life, too bewildered by the speed with which her new universe was unfolding — she just had "so much to do" (Schneller). Now, finally, it's all had a chance to sink in. And Shania Twain, for so long on her way, has finally arrived.

DISCOGRAPHY

Compiled by Bill Borgwardt

ALBUMS

Shania Twain (1993)

1. What Made You Say That. . . . . [2:58]
2. You Lay A Whole Lot Of Love On Me . . . . [2:48]
3. Dance With The One That Brought You . . . . [2:23]
4. Still Under The Weather . . . . [3:06]
5. God Ain't Gonna Getcha For That. . . . . [2:44]
6. Got A Hold On Me. . . . . [2:14]
7. There Goes The Neighborhood. . . . . [3:17]
8. Forget Me . . . . [3:21]
9. When He Leaves You. . . . . [4:21]
10. Crime Of The Century . . . . [3:29]

The Woman In Me (1995)

1. Home Ain't Where His Heart Is (Anymore). . . . . [4:12]
2. Any Man Of Mine . . . . [4:07]
3. Whose Bed Have Your Boots Been Under? . . . . [4:25]
4. (If You're Not In It For Love) I'm Outta Here. . . . . . [4:30]
5. The Woman In Me (Needs The Man In You). . . . . . . [4:50]
6. Is There Life After Love? . . . . [4:39]
7. If It Don't Take Two. . . . . [3:40]
8. You Win My Love . . . . [4:26]
9. Raining On Our Love. . . . . [4:38]
10. Leaving Is The Only Way Out . . . . [4:07]
11. No One Needs To Know. . . . . [3:04]
12. God Bless The Child . . . . [1:30]

The Woman In Me Collector's Edition (1997)

Contains regular "The Woman In Me" CD album plus a bonus
5-track CD "The Radio Remixes"

1. I'm Outta Here (Mutt Lange mix) . . . . [4:21]
2. I'm Outta Here (dance mix) . . . . [4:39]
3. You Win My Love (Mutt mix) . . . . [3:54]
4. God Bless The Child (extended version) . . . . [3:52]
5. The Woman in Me (Needs The Man In You)
    (international acoustic version) . . . . [4:40]

MINI-ALBUMS

U.K. COMMERCIAL CD MINI-ALBUM IN SLIM CASE

Any Man Of Mine (1995)

1. Any Man Of Mine . . . . [4:07]
2. Raining On Our Love. . . . . [4:38]
3. God Ain't Gonna Getcha For That . . . . [2:44]
4. Still Under The Weather . . . . [3:06]

AUSTRALIAN COMMERCIAL CD MINI-ALBUM IN SLIM CASE

The Woman In Me (1995)

1. The Woman In Me (Needs The Man In You)
    (without steel guitar)
2. Whose Bed Have Your Boots Been Under? (dance mix)
3. Leaving Is The Only Way Out (LP version)
4. The Woman In Me (Needs The Man In You) (LP version)

(If You're Not In It For Love) I'm Outta Here
(& remixes) (1996)

1.   I'm Outta Here (Mutt Lange mix). . . . . [4:21]
2.   God Bless The Child (extended version) . . . . [3:48]
3.   I'm Outta Here (dance mix) . . . . [4:40]
4.   I'm Outta Here (album version) . . . . [4:30]
5.   No One Needs To Know. . . . . [3:40]

AUSTRALIAN COMMERCIAL CD
MINI-ALBUM IN CARDBOARD SLIPCASE

You Win My Love (& remix) (1996)

1.   You Win My Love (Mutt mix)
2.   You Win My Love (album version)
3.   If It Don't Take Two
4.   (If You're Not In It For Love) I'm Outta Here

CANADIAN COMMERCIAL CD MINI-ALBUM IN JEWEL CASE

God Bless The Child (1996)

1.   God Bless The Child
     (new previously unreleased version). . . . . [3:49]
2.   (If You're Not In It For Love) I'm Outta Here (remix) [4:40]
3.   Whose Bed Have Your Boots Been Under?
     (dance mix) . . . . [4:50]
4.   The Woman In Me (Needs The Man In You)
     (guitarless mix) . . . . [4:50]

CANADIAN COMMERCIAL CASSETTE
MINI-ALBUM IN JEWEL CASE

God Bless The Child (1996)

1.   God Bless The Child
     (new previously unreleased version). . . . . [3:49]
2.   (If You're Not In It For Love) I'm Outta Here
     (remix) . . . . [4:40]

3. Whose Bed Have Your Boots Been Under?
   (dance mix) .... [4:50]
4. The Woman In Me (Needs The Man In You)
   (guitarless mix) .... [4:50]

SINGLES

What Made You Say That

U.S. PROMOTIONAL CD SINGLE IN JEWEL CASE

What Made You Say That (1993)

1. What Made You Say That .... [2:58]

U.S. COMMERCIAL 7″ SINGLE

What Made You Say That (1993)

1. What Made You Say That .... [2:58]
2. Crime Of The Century........................ [3:24]

Dance With The One That Brought You

U.S. PROMOTIONAL CD SINGLE IN JEWEL CASE

Dance With The One That Brought You (1993)

1. Dance With The One That Brought You .... [2:23]

You Lay A Whole Lot Of Love On Me

U.S. PROMOTIONAL CD SINGLE IN JEWEL CASE

You Lay A Whole Lot Of Love On Me (1993)

1. You Lay A Whole Lot Of Love On Me............ [2:48]

You Lay A Whole Lot Of Love On Me

1. You Lay A Whole Lot Of Love On Me . . . . [2:48]
2. God Ain't Gonna Getcha For That. . . . . [2:44]

U.S. COMMERCIAL 7″ SINGLE

You Lay A Whole Lot of Love On Me (1993)

1. You Lay A Whole Lot Of Love On Me . . . . [2:48]
2. God Ain't Gonna Getcha For That. . . . . [2:44]

Whose Bed Have Your Boots Been Under?

U.S. PROMOTIONAL CD SINGLE IN GATEFOLD COVER

Whose Bed Have Your Boots Been Under? (1994)

1. Whose Bed Have Your Boots Been Under? . . . . [3:58]

U.S. PROMOTIONAL CD SINGLE IN JEWEL CASE

Whose Bed Have Your Boots Been Under? (1994)

1. Whose Bed Have Your Boots Been Under? (dance mix)[4:50]

U.S. COMMERCIAL CD SINGLE IN JEWEL CASE

Whose Bed Have Your Boots Been Under? (1995)

1. Whose Bed Have Your Boots Been Under? (radio) . . . [3:58]
2. Any Man Of Mine . . . . [4:07]
3. Whose Bed Have Your Boots Been Under? (dance mix) . [4:50]

U.S. COMMERCIAL CASSETTE
SINGLE IN CARDBOARD SLIPCASE

Whose Bed Have Your Boots Been Under? (1995)

1. Whose Bed Have Your Boots Been Under? . . . . [3:58]
2. Any Man Of Mine . . . . [4:07]

Whose Bed Have Your Boots Been Under? (1995)

1. Whose Bed Have Your Boots Been Under? . . . . [3:58]
2. Any Man Of Mine . . . . [4:07]

Any Man Of Mine

U.S. PROMOTIONAL CD SINGLE IN GATEFOLD COVER

Any Man Of Mine (1995)

1. Any Man Of Mine . . . . [4:07]

GERMAN PROMOTIONAL CD SINGLE IN SLIM CASE

Any Man Of Mine (1995)

1. Any Man Of Mine . . . . [4:07]

GERMAN COMMERCIAL
CD SINGLE IN CARDBOARD SLIPCASE

Any Man Of Mine (1995)

1. Any Man Of Mine . . . . [4:07]
2. Still Under The Weather . . . . [3:06]

The Woman In Me (Needs The Man In You)

U.S. PROMOTIONAL CD SINGLE IN GATEFOLD COVER

The Woman In Me (Needs The Man In You) (1995)

1. The Woman In Me . . . . [3:57]

MERCURY POLYDOR CANADA PROMOTIONAL CD

This Is Shania Twain — Entertainer Of The Year (1995)

1. The Woman In Me
    (album version: guitarless) . . . . [4:50]

2. You Win My Love . . . . [3:46]
3. (If You're Not In It For Love) I'm Outta Here
   (dance mix) . . . . [4:40]

U.S. COMMERCIAL CD SINGLE
IN CARDBOARD SLIPCASE

The Woman In Me (Needs The Man In You) (1995)

1. The Woman In Me (Needs The Man In You) . . . . [4:50]
2. (If You're Not In It For Love) I'm Outta Here . . . . . . [4:30]

U.S. COMMERCIAL CASSETTE
SINGLE IN CARDBOARD SLIPCASE

The Woman In Me (Needs The Man In You) (1995)

1. The Woman In Me (Needs The Man In You) . . . . [4:50]
2. (If You're Not In It For Love) I'm Outta Here . . . . . . [4:30]

U.S. COMMERCIAL 7″ SINGLE

The Woman In Me (Needs The Man In You) (1995)

1. The Woman In Me (Needs The Man In You) . . . . [4:50]
2. Any Man Of Mine . . . . [4:07]

(If You're Not In It For Love) I'm Outta Here

U.S. PROMOTIONAL CD SINGLE IN GATEFOLD COVER

(If You're Not In It For Love) I'm Outta Here (1995)

1. (If You're Not In It For Love) I'm Outta Here
   (album version) . . . . [4:30]
2. (If You're Not In It For Love) I'm Outta Here
   (edit) . . . . [3:49]
3. (If You're Not In It For Love) I'm Outta Here
   (dance mix) . . . . [4:40]

(If You're Not In It For Love) I'm Outta Here (1995)

1. I'm Outta Here . . . . [4:30]
2. The Woman In Me (Needs The Man In You) . . . . [4:50]

AUSTRALIAN COMMERCIAL CD
SINGLE IN CARDBOARD SLIPCASE

(If You're Not In It For Love) I'm Outta Here (1996)

1. (If You're Not In It For Love) I'm Outta Here
    (Mutt Lange mix) . . . . [4:21]
2. (If You're Not In It For Love) I'm Outta Here
    (dance mix) . . . . [4:40]
3. No One Needs To Know . . . . [3:04]

GERMAN COMMERCIAL 3-TRACK CD SINGLE

(If You're Not In It For Love) I'm Outta Here

[track list unavailable]

U.S. PROMOTIONAL CD SINGLE IN GATEFOLD COVER

(If You're Not In It For Love) I'm Outta Here
(remix) (1996)

1. (If You're Not In It For Love) I'm Outta Here
    (remix) . . . . [4:21]
2. God Bless The Child
    (new previously unreleased version) . . . . [3:48]

U.S. COMMERCIAL CASSETTE
SINGLE IN CARDBOARD SLIPCASE

(If You're Not In It For Love) I'm Outta Here (1996)

1. (If You're Not In It For Love) I'm Outta Here
    (remix) . . . . [4:21]
2. If It Don't Take Two . . . . [3:40]

You Win My Love

U.S. PROMOTIONAL CD SINGLE IN GATEFOLD COVER

You Win My Love (1996)

1.   You Win My Love (edit version) . . . . [3:46]
2.   You Win My Love (edit version) . . . . [3:46]
3.   You Win My Love (album version) . . . . [4:26]

U.S. COMMERCIAL CD SINGLE IN CARDBOARD SLIPCASE

You Win My Love (1995)

1.   You Win My Love . . . . [4:26]
2.   Home Ain't Where His Heart Is (Anymore). . . . . [4:12]

U.S. COMMERCIAL CASSETTE
SINGLE IN CARDBOARD SLIPCASE

You Win My Love (1995)

1.   You Win My Love . . . . [4:26]
2.   Home Ain't Where His Heart Is (Anymore). . . . . [4:12]

U.S. COMMERCIAL 7″ SINGLE

You Win My Love (1995)

1.   You Win My Love . . . . [4:26]
2.   Home Ain't Where His Heart Is (Anymore). . . . . [4:12]

GERMAN COMMERCIAL CD SINGLE — 3 TRACKS

You Win My Love (1995)

[track list unavailable]

AUSTRALIAN COMMERCIAL CD
SINGLE IN CARDBOARD SLIPCASE

You Win My Love (1996)

1.   You Win My Love (Mutt mix)
2.   You Win My Love (album version)
3.   If It Don't Take Two

No One Needs To Know

No One Needs To Know (1996)

1. No One Needs To Know (program plays 3 times) . . . . [3:04]

No One Needs To Know (1995)

1. No One Needs To Know . . . . [3:04]
2. Leaving Is The Only Way Out . . . . [4:07]

Home Ain't Where His Heart Is (Anymore)

Home Ain't Where His Heart Is (Anymore) (1996)

1. Home Ain't Where His Heart Is (Anymore)
   (edit) . . . . [3:59]
2. Home Ain't Where His Heart Is (Anymore)
   (edit) . . . . [3:59]
3. Home Ain't Where His Heart Is (Anymore)
   (album version) . . . . [4:12]

Home Ain't Where His Heart Is (Anymore) (1995)

1. Home Ain't Where His Heart Is (Anymore) . . . . [4:12]
2. Whose Bed Have Your Boots Been Under? . . . . [4:25]

God Bless The Child

God Bless The Child (1996)

1. God Bless The Child
   (new previously unreleased version) . . . . [3:48]
2. (If You're Not In It For Love) I'm Outta Here (remix) [4:21]

God Bless The Child (1996)

1. God Bless The Child
    (new previously unreleased version). . . . . [3:48]
2. (If You're Not In It For Love) I'm Outta Here (remix) [4:21]

U.S. COMMERCIAL CASSETTE
SINGLE IN CARDBOARD SLIPCASE

God Bless The Child (1996)

1. God Bless The Child
    (new previously unreleased version). . . . . [3:48]
2. If It Don't Take Two. . . . . [3:40]

U.S. COMMERCIAL 7″ SINGLE

God Bless The Child (1996)

1. God Bless The Child
    (new previously unreleased version). . . . . [3:48]
2. (If You're Not In It For Love) I'm Outta Here
    (remix) . . . . [4:21]

Love Gets Me Every Time

U.S. COMMERCIAL CD SINGLE IN CARDBOARD SLIPCASE

Love Gets Me Every Time (1997)

1. Love Gets Me Every Time. [3:32]
2. Love Gets Me Every Time (dance mix) . . . . [4:42]

U.S. COMMERCIAL CASSETTE
SINGLE IN CARDBOARD SLIPCASE

Love Gets Me Every Time (1997)

1. Love Gets Me Every Time. [3:32]
2. Love Gets Me Every Time (dance mix) . . . . [4:42]

Love Gets Me Every Time (1997)

1.   Love Gets Me Every Time. . . . . [3:32]
2.   Love Gets Me Every Time (dance mix). . . . . [4:42]

CANADIAN COMMERCIAL CASSETTE SINGLE IN JEWEL CASE

Love Gets Me Every Time (1997)

1.   Love Gets Me Every Time. . . . . [3:32]
2.   Love Gets Me Every Time (dance mix). . . . . [4:42]

COMPILATIONS WITH OTHER ARTISTS

MERCURY PROMOTIONAL CD (1993)

Mercury's Triple Play Sampler (1993)

1.   What Made You Say That . . . . [2:58]
2.   Still Under The Weather . . . . [3:06]
3.   Dance With The One That Brought You . . . . [2:23]
(Also contains 3 tracks each by Toby Keith and John Brannen.)

MERCURY NASHVILLE PROMOTIONAL CD

Music From A New Frontier (1993)

1.   What Made You Say That . . . . [2:58]
(Also contains 7 additional tracks by other Mercury artists.)

MERCURY U.S. PROMOTIONAL CASSETTE

Mercury's Triple Play (1993)

1.   What Made You Say That
2.   Still Under The Weather
(Also contains 2 tracks each by Toby Keith and John Brannen.)

Hot Stuff Volume I (1993)

1. You Lay A Whole Lotta Love On Me . . . . [2:48]
(Also contains tracks by other Mercury artists.)

Should've Been A Single (1993)

1. God Ain't Gonna Getcha For That. . . . . [2:44]
2. Still Under The Weather . . . . [3:06]
(Also contains 2 tracks each by Toby Keith and John Brannen.)

Women Of Country (1994)

1. What Made You Say That
(Also contains 13 other tracks by various female artists.)

The Hot Stuff Volume III (1994)

1. Any Man Of Mine . . . . [4:09]
2. The Woman In Me (Needs The Man In You). . . . . [4:50]
(Also contains 9 other tracks by Mercury artists.)

New Country (January 1995)

1. No One Needs To Know
(Also contains additional tracks by various artists.)

FOCUS (November 1995)

1. I'm Outta Here (radio edit) . . . . [3:49]
(Also contains 19 additional tracks by various artists.)

S
H
A
N
I
A

T
W
A
I
N

CMA — PROMOTIONAL CD

1995 CMA Awards (1995)

1.   Any Man Of Mine
(Also contains 15 other tracks by various country artists.)

MERCURY U.S. PROMOTIONAL CASSETTE

Mercury/Polydor Country Sampler (January 1995)

1.   Whose Bed Have Your Boots Been Under?
(Also contains tracks by other Mercury artists.)

U.S. COMMERCIAL COMPILATION
3-CD BOX SET WITH BOOKLET

50 Years Of Country Music From Mercury (1945–1995)

1.   Any Man Of Mine
(Also contains over 70 tracks from other Mercury artists)

POLYGRAM U.K. COMMERCIAL COMPILATION

The No. 1 Country Album (1996)

1.   Whose Bed Have Your Boots Been Under?
(2-CD set that also contains 43 other tracks by various artists.)

POLYGRAM U.S. COMMERCIAL COMPILATION

Hot Country For The 90's (1996)

1.   Dance With The One That Brought You
(Also contains 11 other tracks by various artists.)

COMMERCIAL COMPILATION CD

1996 Grammy Nominees (1996)

1.   Any Man Of Mine
(Shania was nominated for Best New Artist of 1996. This CD also contains 10 other tracks by various artists.)

CCMA — NCN Fans' Choice Entertainer Of The Year (1996)

1.   I'm Outta Here
(Also contains 4 additional tracks by other nominated artists.)

Twister Motion Picture Soundtrack (1996)

1.   No One Needs To Know
(Also contains 13 additional tracks by various artists.)

Mercury Country Christmas (1996)

1.   God Bless The Child
     (new previously unreleased version). . . . .   [3:48]
2.   God Bless The Child (album version) . . . .   [1:30]
(Also contains 13 additional tracks by various Mercury artists.)

The CMT/Maple Leaf Foods Fans' Choice Award (1997)

1.   No One Needs To Know. . . . .   [3:04]
2.   God Bless The Child . . . .   [1:30]
(Also contains 2 tracks each by Paul Brandt, Terri Clark, Prairie
Oyster, and Michelle Wright)

U.S. PROMOTIONAL CD IN JEWEL CASE

Radio Interview Special (1996)

(Includes God Bless The Child Vignette, plus answers to 5 questions regarding the release of the song and a holiday liner.)

Save The Eagle (1995)

(CD with 30-second public-service announcements by various artists about the American eagle.)

Celebrity Club Liners (December 1995)

(A CD with short spots by celebrities, recorded for use by DJs in clubs; includes 4 tracks by Shania.)

#43 "Doors are closin' soon so drive safe and hurry back!"
#44 "Here's another good rockin' tune by request"
#45 "Take care of your bartenders and waitresses"
#46 "Happy New Year! Countdown" and "Auld Lang Syne"
    by Shania (a cappella)

RADIO SHOWS AND INTERVIEWS

Honky Tonk Sundays #18, 5 Mar. 1995

Featured guest: Shania Twain.

Honky Tonk Sundays #87, 7 July 1996

Featured guest: Shania Twain.

Honky Tonk Sundays #107, 8 Dec. 1996

Christmas memories with "No One Needs To Know," plus short interview clips with Shania and other artists.

Honky Tonk Sundays #114, 26 Jan. 1997

Featured guest: Shania Twain.

Country's Cutting Edge #95-09, 25 Feb. 1995

Featured artist: Shania Twain.

Nashville Record Review #408, 21 and 22 Sept. 1996

Spotlight artist: Shania Twain.

Shania Twain ". . . A Career In High Gear" *Airdate:* 12 Sept. 1996

An SJS entertainment production. Radio show that highlights Shania's career with both interviews and songs.

Country Countdown U.S.A. *Airdate:* weekend of 22 Apr. 1995

Featured in-studio guest: Shania Twain.
A 3-hour country Top 40 countdown show; 3 CDs.
There are many more radio shows with Shania as the featured artist.

BACK-UP VOCALS

Kelita Haverland, **Too Hot To Handle** (1985)

In January 1985, Eileen Twain was at Nashville's Chelsea Studios recording rock demos when Canadian Kelita Haverland asked her if she'd like to sing back-up vocals.

Sammy Kershaw, **Haunted Heart** (1993)

Liner notes have Shania Twain listed as one of four background vocalists.

WORKS CONSULTED

Applebome, Peter. "Grand Ole, Slick New Nashville." *New York Times* 22 Oct. 1995, sec. 5: 8.

"Awards Piling Up on Twain's Mantle." *Daily News* [Halifax] 28 May 1996: 31.

Beck, Marilyn. "Shania Tired of Living out of a Suitcase." *Province* [Vancouver] 22 Apr. 1996: B5.

"Big Twain A-Comin'." *Toronto Sun* 3 May 1996: 80.

Bissley, Jackie. "Shania Twain: Native Ancestry Called into Question." *Windspeaker* May 1996: 8, 15.

Blakey, Rob. "Shania's Star Canine Bowed out of Spotlight." *Calgary Herald* 10 Sept. 1996: D1.

"Born in the U.S.A. Canada." *Broadcaster* Sept. 1995: 17-18.

Brandt, Clark Dominate Canadian Country Awards." *Gazette* [Montreal] 9 Sept. 1997: B5.

Brown, Jim. "Interview with Shania Twain." On-line posting. 31 Mar. 1997.

"Canada's Twain a U.S. Fan Favourite." *Edmonton Journal* 30 Jan. 1996: B6.

Chodan, Lucinda. "La Belle Shania." *Country* July–Aug. 1996: 26–27.

___. "Shania Twain Goes the Distance." *Country* Summer 1993: 10–12.

___. "Shania Twain Takes Quebec by Storm." *Gazette* [Montreal] 5 May 1996: F1.

___. "Twain's World." *Country* Aug. 1995: 10–12.

Cohen, Howard. "With Her Different Background and Sound, Twain's No Typical Country Star." *Knight-Rider/Tribune News Service* 6 Mar. 1996: 1–3.

"Country Music Television Canada Debuts Today." *Calgary Herald* 14 Sept. 1996: C9.

"Country Singer Twain Accused of Ignoring Biological Father." *Gazette* [Montreal] 8 Apr. 1996: B7.

Cruice, Valerie. "From the Racheting of Helecopters to a Guitar's Hum." *New York Times* 8 Dec. 1996: CN13.

Delaney, Larry. "What Made Her Do That!" *Country Music News* May 1993: 1, 11.

___. "Standing Tall: 'Cancountry' Circles the World." *Country Music News* Aug. 1996: 1, 7.

___. Conversation with the author. 19 May 1997.

___. "The Hot Corner." *Country Music News* May 1996: 2.

Dunphy, Catherine. "From Sears Complaint Desk to Stardom." *Toronto Star* 28 Jan. 1996: A1.

"Family Feud: Country Superstar No Native, Her Grandma Reveals." *Province* [Vancouver] 7 Apr. 1996: A26.

Finlay, Liza. "Women Who Rock." *Flare* Apr. 1997: 109–17.

"The Future of Country? Shania Twain a Hit, But Is She the Next Billy Ray Cyrus?" *Daily News* [Halifax] 9 Jan. 1996: 25.

Geocites. "Shania Twain: Biography." On-line posting. 22 Feb. 1997: 1–5.

"Gold Country: Shania Twain." *W5*. CTV Television, 3 June 1996.

Goldsmith, Thomas. "Twain Peaks at Fan Fair." *Country* Aug. 1995: 22.

Goyette, Linda. "An Honor Song for an Ojibwa Superstar: Native Identity Is Not about DNA Tests." *Edmonton Journal* 6 Nov. 1996: A8.

Hager, Barbara. *Honour Song: A Tribute.* Vancouver: Raincoast, 1996.

Hartt, Dave. Telephone interview. 21 June 1997.

Hayden, Rick. "Who Took the Trophies." *Country Weekly* 7 Jan. 1997: 50–54.

Haysom, Ian. "Canadian Singers Have Hit the Big-Time in U.S. Market." *Calgary Herald* 28 Feb. 1996: C4.

Hickey, Bruce. "Twain's Brother Jailed for Hitting Cop, Theft Bid." *Toronto Star* 16 Aug. 1996: D13.

Hitts, Roger. "Shania Twain Helps Fan Fight Back from Killer Crash." *Toronto Star* 1 Apr. 1997: 34.

Howell, Peter. "The Woman in Country Star Feels the Sexes Are Becoming More Compatible." *Toronto Star* 6 Feb. 1996: C4.

Hunter, James. "Black and Blue." *New Country* Feb. 1997: 19–21.

" 'I'm Just Myself': Twain." *Province* [Vancouver] 29 Apr. 1996: B2.

Jennings, Nicholas. "Country Princess." *Maclean's* 28 Aug. 1995: 54–55.

Johnson, Brian D. "Shania Twain: Cinderella of Country." *Maclean's* 18 Dec. 1995: 50–51.

Keyes, John T.D. "On Her Way." *Homemaker's* Nov.–Dec. 1995: 44–45, 47–57.

Kovach, Joelle. "Shania Twain . . . Gets Her 'Day.'" *Country Music News* Oct. 1996: 7.

Krewen, Nick. "Shania's a Golden Gal at Hometown McDonald's." *Country Weekly* 12 Aug. 1997: 11.

___. "There's a Better Album in Me, Says Shania Twain." *Country Weekly* 8 Apr. 1997: 8.

Lague, Louise. "Mark This Twain." *People Weekly* 4 Sept. 1995: 61–62.

Leamer, Laurence. *Three Chords and the Truth.* New York: Harper-Collins, 1997.

Lepage, Mark. "Shania's a Cut Above the Rest." *Country* Apr. 1995: 30.

Liersch, Dawn, and Martha Reyes. "Timmins Honors Twain: Home-town Star Gets Key to City." *Gazette* [Montreal] 16 Aug. 1996: C4.

"Love at First Song." *BC Bookworld* Autumn 1996: 34.

"Low Note for Shania Twain as Second Brother Is Jailed." *National Enquirer* 25 Feb. 1997: 41.

McLaughlin, John P. "Stars on the Rise: Canadian Musicians Are Twanging Their Way into the Hearts of Millions." *Province* [Vancouver] 24 Nov. 1996: B6.

Mitchell, Alison. "Clinton to Celebrate Birthday with Millions from the Coffers." *New York Times* 17 Aug. 1996, sec. 1: 1.

"More Awards for Shania." *Calgary Herald* 24 May 1996: D8.

Muretich, James. "Shania Twain: Reigning Queen of Country Music." *Calgary Herald* 7 Sept. 1996: E10.

Newcomer, Wendy. "How Motown Put Shania on the Road to Nash-ville." *Country Weekly* 4 Mar. 1997: 35.

"No Live Shows for a While as Twain Fears Overexposure." *Edmonton Journal* 17 Mar. 1996: C6.

"Not Easy, Says Twain." *Province* [Vancouver] 28 May 1996: B2.

Ohler, Shawn. "High Noon at the Junos." *Edmonton Journal* 9 Mar. 1996.

"Other Family Criticizes Red-Hot Twain." *Edmonton Journal* 6 Apr. 1996: C6.

Pareles, Jon. "Critic's Notebook: Music Awards for a Mythical Middle." *New York Times* 31 Jan. 1996: C11.

Pasieka, Terry. "Canadian Country: Reaching New Heights." *Network* Oct. 1995: 14–16.

Patterson, Jim. "Shania Twain: The Future of Country?" *Calgary Herald* 9 Jan. 1996: B3.

___. "Twain Kept Waitin': She's Never Won a CMA Award." *Calgary Herald* 28 Sept. 1996: E11.

Phillips, Jill M. "Shania Twain." *Countrybeat* Summer 1997: 43.

Powell, Alison. "Shania Twain." *Interview* Mar. 1996: 102–04.

Press Release. *Shania Twain*, Mercury Records, 1996.

"Producer Stan Campbell Brings New Artists into Recording Studio." *Country Music News* Dec. 1984: 22.

"Radio Airplay Is No Guarantee of Retail Success." *Words and Music* Sept. 1995: 10–12.

Renzetti, Elizabeth. "Dion, the Tragically Hip Dominate Junos." *Globe and Mail* [Toronto] 10 Mar. 1997: C1.

Revkin, Andrew C. "Harmony Rules a Country Music Fair." *New York Times* 15 June 1996, sec. 1: 13.

Richmond, Kay. "I'm Not Faking It." *Country Music International* Aug. 1996: 50–53.

Schneller, Johanna. "Runaway Train." *Chatelaine* May 1996: 56–58.

Schoemer, Karen. "Malling of Shania." *Newsweek* 26 Feb. 1996: 70.

"Shania Doesn't Shy Away from Real Life." *Toronto Sun* 20 Sept. 1997: 44.

"Shania at Ease with Follow-Up." *Calgary Herald* 11 June 1996: C10.

"Shania Goes Home a Star." *Calgary Herald* 16 Aug. 1996: D8.

"Shania in Trouble with Law." *Calgary Herald* 11 Oct. 1996: C3.

"Shania Sitting on Top of the World." *Network* Oct. 1995: 15.

"Shania Snares Rabbits!" *Province* [Vancouver] 17 Mar. 1996: A4.

"Shania to Do SNL, But Controversy over Heritage." *Calgary Herald* 12 Apr. 1996: D3.

"Shania's Alone on the Road." *Calgary Herald* 8 Oct. 1996: D8.

"Shania's Dance Mix Is a Hit in Quebec." *Calgary Herald* 28 Aug. 1996: C9.

"Shania Twain." *Country Music News* Feb. 1997: 1.

"Shania Twain Continues Winning Streak." *Gazette* [Montreal] 27 May 1996: E4.

"Shania Twain Has a Plan B." *Gazette* [Montreal] 4 Apr. 1996: D4.

"Shania Twain: Living the Life of a Country Song." *People Weekly* 25 Dec. 1995: 76.

"Shania Twain: The Metamorphosis of a Star." *Country Music News* Sept. 1995: 20.

"Shania Twain under Attack from Other Family Members." *Calgary Herald* 6 Apr. 1996: C3.

"Shania Twain's Sister Busted for Setting Blaze." *National Enquirer* 18 Mar. 1997: 40.

"Shania Twain's Musical Marriage." *Words and Music* Feb. 1995: 6.

STINFO. "Shania Info." On-line posting. 31 Mar. 1997: 1–3.

Stovall, Natasha. "Pop Briefs." *New York Times* 22 Oct. 1995, sec. 2: 30.

Tarradell, Mario. "Twain's Brothers Arrested." *Daily News* [Halifax] 25 May 1996: 41.

"Thousands of Fans Turn out for Shania Twain." *Toronto Star* 18 Aug. 1996: A6.

"Timmins Turns out for Hometown Star Twain." *Toronto Star* 16 Aug. 1996: D13.

Twain, Shania. "Fan Letter from Shania Twain." *Country* May 1994: 30–31.

____. "Fan Letter: From Shania Twain." *Country* Nov.–Dec. 1995: 30.

"Twain Aiming for That Elusive CMA Trophy." *Daily News* [Halifax] 28 Sept. 1996: 45.

"Twain Best New Artist at American Music Awards." *Gazette* [Montreal] 30 Sept. 1996: D6.

"Twain Brothers Charged in Break-In Bid." *Edmonton Journal* 25 May 1996: C10.

"Twain Campaign Intense." *Gazette* [Montreal] 3 Sept. 1996: F6.

"Twain Finds New Manager." *Province* [Vancouver] 11 Sept. 1996: B4.

"Twain Gets Top Honors at Country Awards." *Daily News* [Halifax] 10 Sept. 1996: 56.

"Twain Hires Springsteen's Manager." *Daily News* [Halifax] 6 Apr. 1996: 25.

"Twain Kin Charged in Bid to Steal Cars." *Toronto Star* 25 May 1996: C11.

"Twain Not Ready to Tour." *Gazette* [Montreal] 18 Mar. 1996: E5.

"Twain Not Truthful on Heritage, Paper Says." *Toronto Star* 6 Apr. 1996: A7.

"Twain on SNL." *Toronto Star* 12 Apr. 1996: D11.

"Twain Promises Deeper Songs." *Daily News* [Halifax] 20 Oct. 1996: 59.

"Twain Returns to Superstar High." *Calgary Herald* 7 Dec. 1996: D9.

"Twain Rise New Twist on Country Scene." *Vancouver Sun* 11 Jan. 1996: C8.

"Twain Says Look Helps Career, But Music Will Keep Her on Top." *Daily News* [Halifax] 6 Feb. 1996: 20.

"Twain Takes Best New Artist Trophy." *Toronto Star* 30 Jan. 1996: C5.

"Twain Violating New York Zoning Laws?" *Daily News* [Halifax] 11 Oct. 1996: 43.

"Twain's Touring Boycott Courts Controversy." *Edmonton Journal* 6 Apr. 1996: 33.

"Twelve Million Reasons Shania's A Hit." *Toronto Sun* 9 Sept. 1997: 1, 44.

"Two More Awards for Twain." *Daily News* [Halifax] 26 Apr. 1996: 33.